Contents

Introduction

● **Welcome to the AA's essential Phrase Books series**, covering the most popular European languages and containing everything you'd expect from a comprehensive language series. They're concise, accessible and easy to understand, and you'll find them indispensable on your trip abroad.

Each guide is divided into 15 themed sections and starts with a pronunciation table which gives you the phonetic spelling to all the words and phrases you'll need to know for your trip, while at the back of the book is an extensive word list and grammar guide which will help you construct basic sentences in your chosen language.

Throughout the book you'll come across coloured boxes with a [icon] beside them. These are designed to help you if you can't understand what your listener is saying to you. Hand the book over to them and encourage them to point to the appropriate answer to the question you are asking.

Other coloured boxes in the book – this time without the symbol – give alphabetical listings of themed words with their English translations beside them.

For extra clarity, we have put all English words and phrases in black, foreign language terms in brown and their phonetic pronunciation in italic.

This phrase book covers all subjects you are likely to come across during the course of your visit, from reserving a room for the night to ordering food and drink at a restaurant and what to do if your car breaks down or you lose your traveller's cheques and money. With over 2,000 commonly used words and essential phrases at your fingertips you can rest assured that you will be able to get by in all situations, so let the essential Phrase Book become your passport to a secure and enjoyable trip!

6

Pronunciation table

The imitated pronunciation should be read as if it were English, bearing in mind the following main points:

Consonants

b, d, f, l, m, n, p, q, t, vk, j, w	as in English			
	rarely appear in Italian			
c	• before **e** and **i**, like **ch** in **ch**ip	*ch*	cinema	*cheenaymah*
	• elsewhere, like **c** in **c**at	*k*	casa	*kahzah*
ch	like **c** in **c**at	*k*	chi	*kee*
g	• before **e** and **i**, like **j** in **j**et	*j*	giro	*jeero*
	• elsewere, like **g** in **g**o	*g*	gatto	*gahtto*
gh	like **g** in **g**o	*gh*	funghi	*foonghee*
gl	• like **lli** in mi**lli**on	*lly*	figlio	*feellyo*
	• (rarely) like **gl** in English	*gl*	inglese	*eenglaysay*
gn	like **ni** in o**ni**on	*n*	bagno	*bahneeo*
h	always silent		ho	*o*
r	trilled like Scottish **r**	*r*	riso	*reezo*
s	• generally like **s** in **s**it	*s*	sette	*sayttay*
	• sometimes like **z** in **z**oo	*z*	rosa	*rozah*
sc	• before e and i, like **sh** in **sh**ot	*sh*	pesce	*payshay*
	• elsewhere, like **sk** in **sk**ip	*sk*	fresco	*fraysko*
z, zz	• generally like **ts** in bi**ts**	*ts*	grazie	*grahtseeay*
	• sometimes like **ds** in moo**ds**	*dz*	zero	*dzayro*

Vowels

a	like **a** in c**a**r	*ah*	**pasta**	*pahstah*
e	like **ay** in w**ay**	*ay*	**sera**	*sayrah*
i	like **ee** in m**ee**t	*ee*	**vini**	*veenee*
o	like **o** in n**o**t	*o*	**notte**	*nottay*
u	like **oo** in f**oo**t	*oo*	**uno**	*oono*

Stressing of words

Stress tends to be on the last syllable but one, e.g. fratello = frah**tay**llo; ragazza = rah**gah**tzah; italiano = eetahlee**ah**no. A number of words have a written accent on the last syllable, to indicate that the final vowel is stressed, e.g. città = cheet**tah**; caffè = kahf**fay**; lunedì = loonay**dee**.

1 Useful lists

1.1 Today or tomorrow?

What day is it today? __	**Oggi, che giorno è?**
	Odjee kay jorno ay?
Today's Monday _____	**Oggi è lunedì**
	Odjee ay loonaydee
– Tuesday _____	**Oggi è martedì**
	Odjee ay mahrtaydee
– Wednesday _____	**Oggi è mercoledì**
	Odjee ay mahrkolaydee
– Thursday_____	**Oggi è giovedì**
	Odjee ay jovaydee
– Friday _____	**Oggi è venerdì**
	Odjee ay vaynahrdee
– Saturday _____	**Oggi è sabato**
	Odjee ay sahbahto
– Sunday _____	**Oggi è domenica**
	Odjee ay domayneekah
in January _____	**in gennaio**
	een jaynnaheeo
since February _____	**da febbraio**
	dah faybbraheeo
in spring_____	**in primavera**
	een preemahvayrah
in summer _____	**in estate/d'estate**
	een aystahtay
in autumn_____	**in autunno**
	een ahootoonno
in winter _____	**in inverno/d'inverno**
	een eenvayrno/deenvayrno
1997 _____	**millenovecentonovantasette**
	meellay/novaychaynto/novahntasayttay
the twentieth century___	**il novecento**
	eel novaychaynto

What's the date today?	Quanti ne abbiamo oggi?
	Kwahntee nay abbeeahmo odjee?
Today's the 24th	Oggi è il ventiquattro
	Odjee ay eel vaynteekwahttro
Monday 3 November 1998	lunedì, tre novembre millenovecentonovantotto
	loonaydee, tray novaymbray meellay/novaychaynto/novahntotto
in the morning	la mattina
	lah mahtteenah
in the afternoon	il pomeriggio
	eel pomayreedjo
in the evening	la sera
	lah sayrah
at night	la notte
	lah nottay
this morning	stamattina
	stahmahtteenah
this afternoon	oggi pomeriggio
	odjee pomayreedjo
this evening	stasera
	stahsayhrah
tonight	stanotte
	stahnottay
last night	la notte scorsa
	lah nottay skorsah
this week	questa settimana
	kwaystah saytteemahnah
next month	il mese prossimo
	eel maysay prosseemo
last year	l'anno scorso
	lahnno skorso
next...	... prossimo/prossima
	... prosseemo/prosseemah

in...days/weeks/ _____	fra... giorni/settimane/mesi/anni
months/years	*frah... jornee/saytteemahnay/*
	mayzee/ahnnee
...weeks ago _____	... settimane fa
	... saytteemahnay fah
day off _____	giorno libero
	jorno leebayro

1.2 Bank holidays

● **The most important** Bank holidays in Italy are the following:

January 1	New Year's Day	Capodanno
January 6	Epiphany	Epifania
March/April	Easter and Easter Monday	Pasqua/Lunedì dell'Angelo
25 April	Liberation Day	Anniversario della Liberazione (1945)
1 May	Labour Day	Festa del lavoro
15 August	Feast of the Assumption	Assunzione (Ferragosto)
1 November	All Saints' Day	Ognissanti
8 December	Feast of the Immaculate Conception	Immacolata Concezione
25 December	Christmas Day	Natale
26 December	Feast of Santo Stefano	Santo Stefano

Most shops, banks and government institutions are closed on these days. Individual towns also have public holidays to celebrate their own patron saints.

1.3 What time is it?

What time is it? _____	Che ore sono?
	Kay oray sono?
It's nine o'clock _____	Sono le nove
	Sono lay novay
– five past ten _____	Sono le dieci e cinque
	Sono lay deeaychy ay cheenkway
– a quarter past eleven _	Sono le undici e un quarto
	Sono lay oondeechee ay oon kwahrto
– twenty past twelve ___	E' mezzogiorno e venti
	Ay maydzojorno ay vayntee
– half past one _____	E' l'una e mezza
	Ay loonah ay maydzah
– twenty-five to three __	Sono le due e trentacinque
	Sono lay dooay ay trayntahcheenkway
– a quarter to four _____	Sono le quattro meno un quarto
	Sono lay kwahttro mayno oon kwahrto
– ten to five _____	Sono le cinque meno dieci
	Sono lay cheenkway mayno deeaychee
It's midday (twelve ____ noon)	E' mezzogiorno
	Ay maydzojorno
It's midnight _____	E' mezzanotte
	Ay maydzahnottay
half an hour _____	una mezz'ora
	oonah maydzorah
What time? _____	A che ora?
	Ah kay orah?
What time can I come _ round?	A che ora potrei venire?
	Ah kay orah potraèe vayneeray?
At... _____	Alle...
	Ahllay...
After... _____	Dopo le...
	Dopo lay...
Before... _____	Prima delle...
	Preemah dayllay...

Between...and... (o'clock)	Fra le... e le... *Frah lay... ay lay...*
From...to...	Dalle... alle... *Dahllay... ahllay...*
In...minutes	Fra... minuti *Frah... meenootee*
– an hour	Fra... un'ora *Frah... oonorah*
–...hours	Fra... ore *Frah...oray*
– a quarter of an hour	Fra un quarto d'ora *Frah oon kwahrto dorah*
– three quarters of an hour	Fra tre quarti d'ora *Frah tray kwahrtèe dorah*
too early/late	troppo presto/tardi *troppo praysto/tahrdee*
on time	in orario/puntuale *een orahreeo/poontooahlay*
summertime (daylight saving)	ora legale *orah laygahlay*
wintertime	ora invernale *orah eenvayrnahlay*

1.4 One, two, three...

0	zero	*dzayro*
1	uno	*oono*
2	due	*dooay*
3	tre	*tray*
4	quattro	*kwahttro*
5	cinque	*cheenkway*
6	sei	*sayèe*
7	sette	*sayttay*
8	otto	*otto*
9	nove	*novay*

10	_____	dieci	*deeaychèe*
11	_____	undici	*oondeechee*
12	_____	dodici	*dodeechee*
13	_____	tredici	*traydeechee*
14	_____	quattordici	*kwahttordeechee*
15	_____	quindici	*kweendeechee*
16	_____	sedici	*saydeechee*
17	_____	diciassette	*deechahssettay*
18	_____	diciotto	*deecheeotto*
19	_____	diciannove	*deechahnnovay*
20	_____	venti	*vayntee*
21	_____	ventuno	*vayntoono*
22	_____	ventidue	*vaynteedooay*
30	_____	trenta	*trayntah*
31	_____	trentuno	*trayntoono*
32	_____	trentadue	*trayntahdooay*
40	_____	quaranta	*kwahrahntah*
50	_____	cinquanta	*cheenkwahntah*
60	_____	sessanta	*sayssahntah*
70	_____	settanta	*sayttahntah*
80	_____	ottanta	*ottahntah*
90	_____	novanta	*novahntah*
100	_____	cento	*chaynto*
101	_____	centouno	*chayntooono*
110	_____	centodieci	*chayntodeeaychee*
120	_____	centoventi	*chayntovayntee*
200	_____	duecento	*dooaychaynto*
300	_____	trecento	*traychaynto*
400	_____	quattrocento	*kwahttrochaynto*
500	_____	cinquecento	*cheenkwaychaynto*
600	_____	seicento	*saychaynto*
700	_____	settecento	*sayttaychaynto*
800	_____	ottocento	*ottochaynto*
900	_____	novecento	*novaychaynto*
1,000	_____	mille	*meellay*

1,100 _____	millecento	*meellaychaynto*
2,000 _____	duemila	*dooaymeelah*
10,000 _____	diecimila	*deeaycheemeelah*
100,000 _____	centomila	*chayntomeelah*
1,000,000 _____	un milione	*oon meeleeonay*
1st _____	primo	*preemo*
2nd _____	secondo	*saykondo*
3rd _____	terzo	*tayrtzo*
4th _____	quarto	*kwahrto*
5th _____	quinto	*kweento*
6th _____	sesto	*saysto*
7th _____	settimo	*saytteemo*
8th _____	ottavo	*ottahvo*
9th _____	nono	*nono*
10th _____	decimo	*daycheemo*
11th _____	undicesimo	*oondeechayzeemo*
12th _____	dodicesimo	*dodeechayzeemo*
13th _____	tredicesimo	*traydeechayzeemo*
14th _____	quattordicesimo	*kwahttordeechayzeemo*
15th _____	quindicesimo	*kweendeechayzeemo*
16th _____	sedicesimo	*saydeechayzeemo*
17th _____	diciassettesimo	*deechahsayttayzeemo*
18th _____	diciottesimo	*deechottayzeemo*
19th _____	diciannovesimo	*deechahnovayzeemo*
20th _____	ventesimo	*vayntayzeemo*
21st _____	ventunesimo	*vayntoonayzeemo*
22nd _____	ventiduesimo	*vaynteedooayzeemo*
30th _____	trentesimo	*trahntayzeemo*
100th _____	centesimo	*chayntayzeemo*
1,000th _____	millesimo	*meellayzeemo*
once _____	una volta	*oonah voltah*
twice _____	due volte	*dooay voltay*

double _____	il doppio	*eel doppeeo*
triple _____	il triplo	*eel treeplo*
half _____	la metà	*lah maytah*
a quarter _____	un quarto	*oon kwahrto*
a third _____	un terzo	*oon tayrtzo*
some/a few _____	alcuni	*ahlkoonee*

2 + 4 = 6 _____ due più quattro fa sei
dooay peeoo kwahttro fah sayèe

4 - 2 = 2 _____ quattro meno due fa due
kwahttro mayno dooay fah dooay

2 x 4 = 8 _____ due per quattro fa otto
dooay payr kwahttro fah otto

4 ÷ 2 = 2 _____ quattro diviso due fa due
kwahttro deeveezo dooay fah dooay

even/odd _____ pari/dispari
pahree/deesparee

total_____ (in) totale
(een) totahlay

6 x 9 _____ sei per nove
sayèe payr novay

1.5 The weather

Is the weather going ___ **Avremo bel/cattivo tempo?**
to be good/bad? *Avraymo bayl/kahtteevo taympo?*

Is it going to get _____ **Farà più freddo/più caldo?**
colder/hotter? *Fahrah peeoo frayddo/peeoo kahldo?*

What temperature is it__ **Quanti gradi ci saranno?**
going to be? *Kwahntee grahdee chee sahrahnno?*

Is it going to rain? _____ **Pioverà?**
Peeovayrah?

afoso sweltering/muggy
assolato sunny
bello fine
brina frost/frosty
caldissimo very hot
diluvio heavy rain
forza del vento moderata/forte/ molto forte moderate/strong/very strong winds
freddo umido cold and damp
fresco cool
gelido bleak
gelo frost

gelo notturno overnight frost
ghiaccio ice/icy
giornata di sole sunny day
... gradi (sotto/sopra zero) ... degrees (below/above zero)
grandine hail
mite mild
nebbia fog/foggy
neve snow
nuvolosità cloudiness
ondata di caldo heatwave

pioggia rain
raffiche di vento gusts of wind
rovescio di pioggia downpour
sereno/nuvoloso/coperto clear skies/cloudy/overcast
sereno fine/clear
soffocante stifling
tempesta storm
umido humid
uragano hurricaine
vento wind
ventoso windy

Is there going to be a ___ storm?	Ci sarà una tempesta?	*Chee sahrah oonah taympaystah?*
Is it going to snow? _____	Nevicherà?	*Nayveekayrah?*
Is it going to freeze? ___	Gelerà?	*Jaylayrah?*
Is the thaw setting in? __	Sgelerà?	*Sjaylayrah?*
Is it going to be foggy? _	Ci sarà la nebbia?	*Chee sahrah lah naybbeeah?*
Is there going to be a ___ thunderstorm?	Avremo un temporale?	*Ahvraymo oon taymporahlay?*
The weather's changing	Il tempo cambia	*Eel taympo kahmbeeah*

It's going to be cold____	Farà freddo
	Fahrah frayddo
What's the weather ____ going to be like today/ tomorrow?	Che tempo farà oggi/domani?
	Kay taympo fahrah odjee/domahnee?

1.6 Here, there...

See also 5.1 Asking for directions

here, over here/there, over there	qui, qua/lì, là
	kwee, kwah/lee, lah
somewhere/nowhere ____	da qualche parte/da nessuna parte
	dah kwahlkay pahrtay/dah nayssoonah pahrtay
everywhere _____	dappertutto
	dahppayrtootto
far away/nearby _____	lontano/vicino
	lontahno/veecheeno
(on the) right/(on the) left	a destra/a sinistra
	ah daystrah/ah seeneestrah
to the right/left of _____	a destra di/a sinistra di
	ah daystrah dee/ah seeneestrah dee
straight ahead_____	dritto
	dreetto
via _____	per
	payr
in/to _____	in/a
	een/ah
on _____	su/sopra
	soo/soprah
under _____	sotto
	sotto
against _____	contro
	contro

opposite/facing_____	**di fronte a**
	dee frontay ah
next to _____	**accanto a**
	ahkkahnto ah
near_____	**presso/vicino a**
	praysso/veecheeno ah
in front of_____	**davanti a/dinanzi a**
	dahvahntee ah/deenahnzee ah
in the centre _____	**al centro**
	al chayntro
forward_____	**avanti**
	ahvahntee
down_____	**(in) giù**
	(een) joo
up _____	**(in) su**
	(een) soo
inside _____	**dentro**
	dayntro
outside _____	**fuori**
	fworee
behind _____	**(in) dietro**
	(een) deeayhtro
at the front_____	**davanti**
	dahvahntee
at the back/in line _____	**in fondo/in fila**
	een fondo/een feelah
in the north _____	**nel nord**
	nayl nord
to the south_____	**al sud**
	ahl sood
from the west _____	**dall'ovest**
	dahllovayst
from the east_____	**dall'est**
	dahllayst
to the...of _____	**a... di**
	ah... dee

1.7 What does that sign say?

See also 5.4 Traffic signs

a noleggio for hire
acqua calda/fredda hot/cold water
acqua (non) potabile (no) drinking water
affittasi for rent
albergo hotel
alt stop
alta tensione high voltage
aperto open
attenti al cane beware of the dog
attenzione danger
biglietteria ticket office
cambio exchange
carabinieri police
cassa cash desk/pay here
chiuso (per ferie/restauro) closed (for holiday/refurbishment)
completo full
divieto di caccia/pesca no hunting/fishing
entrata entrance
esaurito sold out
freno d'emergenza hand brake

fuori uso not in use
gabinetti lavatories/toilets
guasto out of order
in vendita for sale
informazioni information
ingresso (libero) entrance (free)
non disturbare/toccare please do not disturb/touch
occupato engaged
orario timetable
ospedale hospital
pedoni pedestrians
pericolo (d'incendio/di morte) danger/fire hazard/danger to life
polizia stradale traffic police
pronto soccorso first aid/accident and emergency (hospital)
riservato reserved
sala d'attesa waiting room

scala di sicurezza/mobile fire escape/escalator
spingere push
tirare pull
ufficio informazioni turistiche tourist information bureau
ufficio postale post office
uscita (di emergenza) (emergency) exit
vendesi for sale
vernice fresca wet paint
vietato fumare/gettare rifiuti no smoking/no litter
vietato l'accesso/l'ingresso no access/no entry
vigili del fuoco fire brigade
vigili urbani (municipal) police

1.8 Telephone alphabet

Pronouncing the alphabet, e.g. A as in Ancona

a	*ah*	come Ancona	*komay Ankonah*
b	*bee*	come Bologna	*komay Bolonyah*
c	*chee*	come Como	*komay Komo*
d	*dee*	come Domodossola	*komay Domodossolah*
e	*ay*	come Empoli	*komay Empolee*
f	*ayffay*	come Firenze	*komay Feeraynzay*
g	*jee*	come Genova	*komay Jaynovah*
h	*ahkkah*	come Hotel	*komay Hotayl*
i	*ee*	come Imola	*komay Eemolah*
j	*ee loongo*	come Jersey	*komay Jayrsay*
k	*kahppah*	come Kursaal	*komay Koorsaal*
l	*ayllay*	come Livorno	*komay Leevorno*
m	*aymmay*	come Milano	*komay Meelahno*
n	*aynnay*	come Napoli	*komay Nahpolee*
o	*o*	come Otranto	*komay Otrahnto*
p	*pee*	come Padova	*komay Pahdovah*
q	*koo*	come Quarto	*komay Kwahrto*
r	*ayrray*	come Roma	*komay Romah*
s	*ayssay*	come Savona	*komay Sahvonah*
t	*tee*	come Torino	*komay Toreeno*
u	*oo*	come Udine	*komay Oodeenay*
v	*voo*	come Venezia	*komay Vaynaytzyah*
w	*doppeeovoo*	come Washington	*komay Washington*
	or voodoppeeo		
x	*eex*	come Xeres	*komay Xayrays*
y	*eepseelon*	come York, yacht	*komay York, yahcht*
z	*dzayhtah*	come Zara	*komay Dzahrah*

1.9 Personal details

surname _____ cognome
koneeomay

first/forename _____ nome *nomay*

initials _____ iniziali *eeneetzeeahlee*

address (street/ _____ indirizzo (via/numero)
number) *eendeereetzo (veeah/noomahro)*

post code/town _____ codice postale/residenza
kodeechay postahlay/rayseedayntzah

sex (male/female)_____ sesso (m/f)
saysso (m/f)

nationality/citizenship __ nazionalità/cittadinanza
nahtzeeonahleetah/cheettahdeenahntzah

date of birth_____ data di nascita
dahtah dee nahsheetah

place of birth_____ luogo di nascita
loo-ogo dee nahsheetah

occupation _____ professione
profaysseeonay

marital status _____ stato civile
stahto cheeveelay

married, single _____ coniugato/a, celibe (m) nubile (f)
konyoogahto/tah, chayleebay/ noobeelay

widowed _____ vedovo (m), vedova (f)
vaydovo, vaydovah

(number of) children_____ (numero di) figli
(noomahro dee) feelly

passport/identity _____ numero del passaporto/della carta di
card/driving licence   identità/della patente
number *noomayro dayl pahssahporto/dayllah
cahrtah deedaynteetah/dayllah pahtayntay*

place and date of _____ luogo e data di rilascio
issue *loo-ogo ay dahtah dee reelahshyo*

signature _____ firma
feermah

2 Courtesies

● **It is usual in Italy** to shake hands on meeting and parting company. Female friends and relatives may kiss each other on both cheeks when meeting and parting company. For men, this is also quite usual. It is also polite to say *Signore* and *Signora* quite systematically as part of a greeting, i.e. *Buongiorno/arrivederLa, signora*.

2.1 Greetings

Hello/Good morning ___ Mr Williams	**Buongiorno signor Williams** *Bwonjorno seeneeor Williams*
Hello/Good morning ___ Mrs Jones	**Buongiorno signora Jones** *Bwonjorno sineeorah Jones*
Hello, Peter _____	**Ciao Peter** *Chaho Peter*
Hi, Helen _____	**Ciao Helen** *Chaho Helen*
Good morning, madam_	**Buongiorno signora** *Bwonjorno seeneeorah*
Good afternoon, sir ____	**Buongiorno signore** *Bwonjorno seeneeoray*
Good afternoon/ _____ evening	**Buona sera** *Bwona sayrah*
Hello/Good morning ___	**Buongiorno** *Bwonjorno*
How are you?/How are _ things?	**Come va?** *Komay vah?*
Fine, thank you, _____ and you?	**Bene, grazie, e Lei?** *Baynay, grahtzeeay, ay layee?*
Very well, and you? ____	**Benissimo, e Lei?** *Bayneesseemo, ay layee?*
In excellent health/_____ In great shape	**In ottima forma** *Een otteemah formah*
So-so _____	**Così così** *Cozee cozee*

Not very well _____	**Non molto bene**
	Non molto baynay
Not bad _____	**Non c'è male**
	Non chay mahlay
I'm going to leave _____	**Me ne vado**
	May nay vahdo
I have to be going _____ someone's waiting for me	**Devo andarmene. Mi aspettano**
	Dayvo ahndahrmaynay. Mee ahspettahno
Goodbye _____	**Ciao!**
	Chaho!
Good-bye/Good-bye ___ (formal)/See you later	**Arrivederci/ArrivederLa/Ci vediamo**
	Ahrreevaydayrchee/ahrreevaydayrlah/chee vaydeeahmo
See you soon _____	**A presto**
	Ah praysto
See you later_____	**A più tardi**
	Ah peeoo tahrdee
See you in a little while _	**A fra poco**
	Ah frah poko
Sweet dreams_____	**Sogni d'oro**
	Sonyee doro
Good night _____	**Buona notte**
	Bwonah nottay
All the best _____	**Tante belle cose**
	Tahntay bayllay kozay
Have fun _____	**Buon divertimento**
	Bwon deevayrteemaynto
Good luck _____	**Buona fortuna/in bocca al lupo**
	Bwonah fortoonah/een bokkah al loopo
Have a nice holiday ____	**Buone vacanze/buone ferie**
	Bwonay vahkahntzay/bwonay fayreeay
Bon voyage/Have a ___ good trip	**Buon viaggio**
	Bwon veeahdjo
Thank you, the same___ to you	**Grazie, altrettanto**
	Grahtzeeay, ahltrayttahnto

Say hello to/Give my ___   **Mi saluti...**
  regards to (formal)....   *Mee sahlootee...*
Say hello to (informal) __   **Salutami...**
    Sahlootahmee...

2.2 How to ask a question

Who? _____	**Chi?**
	Kee?
Who's that?/Who is ____	**Chi è?**
it?/Who's there?	*Kee ay?*
What?_____	**Che (cosa)?**
	Kay (kosah)?
What is there to _____	**Che c'è da vedere?**
see?	*Kay chay dah vaydayray?*
What category of hotel _	**Che tipo di albergo è?**
is it?	*Kay teepo dee ahlbayrgo ay?*
Where?_____	**Dove?**
	Dovay?
Where's the_____	**Dov'è il bagno?**
toilet/bathroom?	*Dovay ay eel bahneeo?*
Where are you going? __	**Dove va?**
(formal)	*Dovay vah?*
Where are you from? ___	**Da dove viene?**
	Dah dovay veeayhnay?
What?/How? _____	**Come?**
	Komay?
How far is that? _____	**Quanto è lontano?**
	Kwahnto ay lontahno?
How long does _____	**Quanto tempo ci vorrà?**
that take?	*Kwahnto taympo chee vorrah?*
How long is the trip? ___	**Quanto tempo durerà il viaggio?**
	Kwahnto taympo doorayrah eel veeahhdjo?
How much?_____	**Quanto?**
	Kwahnto?

How much is this? _____	Quanto costa?
	Kwahnto kostah?
What time is it? _____	Che ore sono?
	Kay oray sono?
Which one/s? _____	Quale?/Quali?
	Kwahlay?/Kwahlee?
Which glass is mine? __	Qual è il mio bicchiere?
	Kwahlay eel meeo beekkeeayray?
When? _____	Quando?
	Kwahndo?
When are you leaving? _	Quando parte?
(formal)	*Kwahndo pahrtay?*
Why? _____	Perchè?
	Payrkay?
Could you...? (formal) __	Potrebbe...?
	Potraybbay..?
Could you help me/ ____	Potrebbe darmi una mano, per piacere?
give me a hand	*Potraybbay dahrmee oonah mahno, payr*
please?	*peeahchayray?*
Could you point that __	Potrebbe indicarmelo?
out to me/show me	*Potraybbay eendeekahrmayhlo?*
please?	
Could you come_____	Potrebbe accompagnarmi, per favore?
with me, please?	*Potraybbay ahkkompahnyahrmee, payr*
	fahvoray?
Could you reserve/ ____	Mi potrebbe prenotare dei biglietti, per
book me some	piacere?
tickets please?	*Mee potraybbay praynotahray day*
	beellyayttee, payr peeahchayray?
Could you recommend _	Saprebbe consigliarmi un altro albergo?
another hotel?	*Sahpraybbay konseellyahrmee oonahltro*
	ahlbayrgo?
Do you know...? _____	Saprebbe...?
(formal)	*Saprebbay...?*
Do you know _____	Sa se...?
whether...?	*Sah say...?*

Do you have...? (formal)	Ha...? *Ah...?*
Do you have a.... for me?	Ha un/una... per me? *Ah oon/oona..... payr may?*
Do you have a vegetarian dish, please?	Ha per caso un piatto vegetariano/senza carne? *Ah payr kahzo oon pyahtto vayjaytahryahno/saynzah kahrnay?*
I would like...	Vorrei... *Vorrayee...*
I'd like a kilo of apples, please	Vorrei un chilo di mele *Vorrayee oon keelo dee mayhlay*
Can/May I?	Posso...? *Posso...?*
Can/May I take this away?	Posso portare via questo? *Posso portahray veeah kwaysto?*
Can I smoke here?	Si può fumare qui? *See pwo foomahray kwee?*
Could I ask you something?	Posso farLe una domanda? *Posso fahrlay oonah domahndah?*

2.3 How to reply

Yes, of course	Sì certo *See chayrto*
No, I'm sorry	No, mi dispiace *No, mee deespeeahchay*
Yes, what can I do for you?	Sì, che cosa desidera? *See, kay kosah dayzeederah?*
Just a moment, please	Un attimo, per favore *Oon attymo payr fahvoray*
No, I don't have time now	No, purtroppo ora non ho tempo *No, poortroppo orah non o taympo*
No, that's impossible	No, non è possibile *No, non ay posseebeelay*

I think so/I think that's___ absolutely right	Credo di sì/Credo proprio di sì
	Kraydo dee see/Kraydo propreeo dee see
I think so too/I agree ___	Lo penso anch'io
	Lo paynso ahnkeeo
I hope so too_____	Lo spero anch'io
	Lo spayro ankeeo
No, not at all/ _____ Absolutely not	No, niente affatto
	No, neeayntay ahffahtto
No, no-one _____	No, nessuno
	No, nayssoono
No, nothing _____	No, niente
	No, neeayntay
That's right _____	Esatto
	Ezahtto
Something's wrong ____	C'è qualcosa che non va
	Chay kwahlkosah kahy non vah
I agree (don't agree) ___	(Non) sono d'accordo
	(Non) sono dahkkordo
OK/it's fine _____	Va bene
	Vah bayhnay
OK, all right_____	D'accordo
	Dahkkordo
Perhaps/maybe _____	Forse
	Forsay
I don't know _____	Non lo so
	Non lo so

2.4 Thank you

Thank you _____	Grazie
	Grahtzeeay
You're welcome _____	Di niente/nulla
	Dee neeayntay/noollah
Thank you very much/ _ Many thanks	Mille grazie
	Meellay grahtzeeay

Very kind of you _____	**Molto gentile**
	Molto jaynteelay
My pleasure_____	**E' stato un piacere**
	Ay stahto oon peeahchayray
I enjoyed it very much__	**Mi è piaciuto moltissimo**
	Mee ay peeacheeooto molteesseemo
Thank you for..._____	**La ringrazio di...**
	Lah reengrahtzeeo dee...
You shouldn't have/That was so kind of you	**E stato veramente gentile/da parte sua**
	Ay stahto vayrahmayntay jaynteelay/dah pahrtay sooah
Don't mention it!_____	**Ma si figuri!**
	Mah see feegoory!
That's all right _____	**Prego**
	Praygo

2.5 Sorry

Excuse me/pardon_____ me/sorry (formal)	**Scusi!**
	Skoozee!
Excuse me/pardon_____ me/sorry (informal)	**Scusa!**
	Skoozah!
Sorry, I didn't know _____ that....	**Scusi, ma non sapevo che...**
	Skoozee, mah non sahpayvo kay...
Excuse/pardon me_____ (formal)	**Mi scusi**
	Mee skoozee
I do apologise _____ (formal/informal)	**La/ti prego di scusarmi**
	Lah/tee praygo dee scoosahrmee
I'm sorry_____	**Mi dispiace**
	Mee deespeeahchay
I didn't mean it/It was __ an accident	**Non l'ho fatto apposta**
	Non lo fahtto appostah
That's all right/Don't ___ worry about it (formal)	**Non si preoccupi**
	Non see prayokkoopee

Never mind/Forget it ___ (informal)	Non importa *Non eemportah*
It could happen to _____ anyone	Può succedere a tutti *Pwo sootchaydayray ah tootty*

2.6 What do you think?

Which do you prefer/like best (formal)	Cosa preferisce? *Kosah prayfayreeshay?*
What do you think? ___ (informal)	Che ne pensi? *Kay nay pensee?*
Don't you like dancing? (formal/informal)	Non le/ti piace ballare? *Non lay/tee peeahchay bahllahray?*
I don't mind_____	Per me è uguale *Payr may ay oogwahlay*
Well done! (m.sing/ _____ f.sing/m.plu/f.plu)	Bravo/brava/bravi/brave! *Brahvo/brahvah/brahvee/brahvay!*
Not bad!_____	Niente male! *Neeayntay mahlay!*
Great!/Marvellous! _____	Che meraviglia! *Kay mayrahveellyah!*
Wonderful! _____	Stupendo! *Stoopayndo!*
How lovely! _____	Che bello! *Kay bayllo!*
I am pleased for you ___ (formal/informal)	Mi fa piacere per Lei/te *Mee fah peeahchay payr layee/tay*
I'm (not very happy)_____ delighted to/with...	(Non) sono molto contento/a di... *(Non) sono molto contaynto/ah dee...*
It's really nice here! ____	È proprio un bel posto *Ay propreeo oon bayl posto*
How nice!_____	Che bello! *Kay bayllo!*
How nice for you!_____	Mi fa piacere per Lei/te *Mee fah peeahchayray payr Layee/tay*

I'm (not) very happy with...	(Non) sono molto contento/a di *(Non) sono molto kontaynto/ah dee*
I'm glad that....	Sono contento che... *Sono kontaynto kay...*
I'm having a great time	Mi sto divertendo moltissimo *Mee sto deevayrtayndo molteesseemo*
I can't wait 'til tomorrow/I'm looking forward to tomorrow	Non vedo l'ora che sia domani *Non vaydo lorah kay seeah domahny*
I hope it works out	Spero che vada bene *Spayhro kay vahdah bayhnay*
How awful!	Che brutto! *Kay brootto!*
It's horrible	E' orribile *Ay orreebeelay*
That's ridiculous!	È ridicolo! *Ay reedeekolo!*
That's terrible!	Ma è terribile! *Mah ay tayrreebeelay!*
What a pity/shame!	Che peccato! *Kay paykkahto!*
How disgusting!	Che schifo! *Kay skeefo!*
What a load of rubbish/How silly!	Che sciocchezze! *Kay shokkaytzay!*
I don't like it/them	Non mi piace.../Non mi piacciono... *Non mee peeahchay.../Non mee peeahcheeono...*
I'm bored to death	Sto morendo di noia *Sto morayndo dee noeeah*
I'm fed up	Mi sono stufato/a *Mee sono stoofahto/ah*
This is no good	Questo non va bene *Kwaysto non vah baynay*
This is not what I expected	Mi aspettavo una cosa diversa *Mee ahspayttahvo oonah kosah deevayrsah*

3

Conversation

3.1 I beg your pardon?

I don't speak any/ _____ I speak a little...	Non parlo/Parlo un po' di... *Non parlo/Parlo oon po dee...*
I'm English_____	Sono inglese *Sono eenglaysay*
I'm Scottish_____	Sono scozzese *Sono skotzaysay*
I'm Irish _____	Sono irlandese *Sono eerlahndaysay*
I'm Welsh_____	Sono gallese *Sono gahllaysay*
Do you speak English? _ (formal)	Lei parla inglese? *Layee pahrlah eenglaysay?*
Is there anyone who _____ speaks...?	C'è qualcuno che parla...? *Chay kwahlkoono kay pahrlah...?*
I beg your pardon/_____ What?	Come? *Komay?*
I (don't) understand _____	(Non) capisco *(Non) kahpeesko*
Do you understand _____ me? (formal)	Mi capisce? *Mee kahpeeshay?*
Could you repeat that, _ please?	Potrebbe ripetermelo? *Potraybbay reepayhtayrmaylo?*
Could you speak more _ slowly, please?	Potrebbe parlare un po' più lentamente? *Potraybbay pahrlahray oon po peeoo layntahmayntay?*
What does that _____ mean?/that word mean?	Che cosa significa/Che cosa significa quella parola? *Kay kosah seeneefeekah/Kay kosah seeneefeekah kwayllah pahrolah?*
It's more or less the_____ same as...	E' più o meno lo stesso di...? *Ay peeoo o mayno lo staysso dee..*
Could you write that _____ down for me, please?	Potrebbe scrivermelo? *Potraybbay skreevayrmaylo?*

Could you spell that for me, please?	Come si scrive?
	Komay see skreevay?

(See 1.8 Telephone alphabet)

Could you point that out in this phrase book, please?	Potrebbe indicarmelo in questo frasario?
	Potraybbay eendeekahrmaylo een kwaysto frahzahreeo?
Just a minute, I'll look it up	Un attimo che lo cerco
	Oon ahtteemo kay lo chayrko
I can't find the word/ the sentence	Non riesco a trovare la parola/la frase
	Non reeaysko ah trovahray lah pahrolah/lah frahzay
How do you say that in...?	Come si dice in...?
	Komay see deechay een...?
How do you pronounce that?	Come si pronuncia?
	Komay see pronoonchah?

3.2 Introductions

May I introduce myself?	Permette che mi presenti?
	Payrmayttay kay mee praysayntee?
My name's...	Mi chiamo...
	Mee keeahmo...
I'm...	Sono...
	Sono...
What's your name? (formal/informal)...	Lei, come si chiama?/Come ti chiami?
	Lay, komay see keeahmah?/Komay tee keeahmee?
May I introduce...? (formal/informal)...	Permette, Le presento.../Permetti, ti presento...
	Payrmayttay, lay praysaynto.../Payrmayttee, tee praysaynto...

This is my wife/ husband (formal/informal)	Le/ti presento mia moglie/mio marito
	Lay/tee praysaynto meeah mollyay/meeo mahreeto
This is my daughter/ son (formal/informal)	Le/ti presento mia figlia/mio figlio
	Lay/tee presento meeah feellyah/meeo feellyo
This is my mother/ father (formal/informal)	Le/ti presento mia madre/mio padre
	Lay/tee praysaynto meeah mahdray/meeo pahdray
This is my fiancée/fiancé (formal/informal)	Le/ti presento la mia fidanzata/il mio fidanzato
	Lay/tee praysaynto lah meeah feedahntzahtah/eel meeo feedahntzahto
This is my friend (f/m) (formal/informal)	Le/ti presento un'amica mia/un amico mio
	Lay/tee praysaynto oonahmeekah meeah/oonahmeeko meeo
How do you do	Piacere
	Peeahchayray
Hi, pleased to meet you (informal)	Ciao, piacere di conoscerti
	Chahoo, peeahchayray dee konoshayrtee
Pleased to meet you (formal)	Piacere di conoscerLa
	Peeahchayray dee konoshayrlah
Where are you from? (formal/informal)	Lei, di dov'è?/Di dove sei?
	Layèe dee dovay ay?/Dee dovay sayee?
I'm English	Sono inglese
	Sono eenglaysay
What city do you live in?	In quale città abita?
	Een kwahlay cheettah ahbeetah?
In...near....	Abito a... vicino a...
	Ahbeeto ah... veecheeno ah...
Have you been here long?	E' molto che sta qui?
	Ay molto kay stah kwee?
A few days	Qualche giorno
	Kwahlkay jorno
How long are you staying here?	Quanto tempo rimarrà?
	Kwahnto taympo reemahrrah?

We're (probably) _____ leaving tomorrow/ in two weeks	Partiremo (probabilmente) domani/fra due settimane
	Pahrtyraymo (probahbeelmayntay) domahny/frah dooay sayttymahnay
Where are you (m/f) ___ staying?	Dov'è alloggiato/a?
	Dovay ay ahllodjahto/ah?
I'm staying in a hotel/ __ an apartment	Sono alloggiato in un albergo/ appartamento
	Sono ahllodjahto een oon ahlbayrgo/ahppahrtahmaynto
At a campsite _____	Sono in campeggio
	Sono een kahmpaydjo
I'm staying with _____ friends/relatives	Sono ospite di amici/sono a casa di parenti
	Sono ospeetay dee ahmeechee/sono ah kasa dee pahrayntee
Are you (m/f) here on___ your own? Are you here with your family?	E' da solo/a?/E' con la Sua famiglia?
	Ay dah solo/ah?/Ay con lah sooah fahmeellyah?
I'm on my own _____	Sono da solo/a
	Sono dah solo/ah
I'm with my _____ partner/wife/husband	Sono con il mio partner/la mia partner/mia moglie/mio marito
	Sono con eel meeo pahrtnayr/lah meeah pahrtnayr/meeah mollyay/meeo mahreeto
– with my family _____	Sono con la mia famiglia
	Sono con lah meeah fahmeellyah
– with relatives _____	Sono con i miei parenti
	Sono con ee meeayee pahrayntee
– with a friend/friends __ (m.sing/f.sing/m. plu/ f.plu)	Sono con un amico/un'amica/degli amici/delle amiche
	Sono con oonahmeeko/oonahmeekah/ daylyee ahmeechee/daylly ahmeekay
Are you married? (m/f) _	Lei è sposato/a?
	Layèe ay sposahto/ah?

Are you engaged?/ Do you have a steady boy/girlfriend?	È fidanzato/È fidanzata? *Ay feedahntzahto/Ay feedahntzahtah?*
That's none of your business (formal/informal)	Questo non La/ti riguarda per niente *Kwaysto non lah/tee reegwahrdah payr nee-ayntay*
I'm married (m/f)	Sono sposato/a *Sono spozahto/ah*
I'm single (m. only)	Sono scapolo *Sono skahpolo*
I'm not married (m/f)	Non sono sposato/a *Non sono sposahto/ah*
I'm separated (m/f)	Sono separato/a *Sono saypahrahto/ah*
I'm divorced (m/f)	Sono divorziato/a *Sono deevortzeeahto/ah*
I'm a widow/widower	Sono vedova/o *Sono vaydovah/o*
I live alone (m/f)/with someone	Vivo da solo/a/Vivo con il mio partner/la mia partner *Veevo dah solo/ah/Veevo con eel meeo pahrtnayr/lah meeah pahrtnayr*
Do you have any children/grandchildren?	Ha figli/nipoti? *Ah feelly/neepotee?*
How old are (formal/informal) you?	Quanti anni ha/hai? *Kwahnty ahnnee ah/ahee?*
How old is she/he?	Quanti anni ha (lei/lui)? *Kwahnty ahnnee ah (lahee/looee)?*
I'm... (years old)	Ho...anni *O...ahnnee*
She's/he's...(years old)	Ha...anni *Ah...ahnnee*
What do you do for a living? (formal/informal)	Che lavoro fa/fai?? *Kay lahvoro faah?/faee?*
I work in an office	Lavoro in ufficio *Lahvoro een ooffeecho*

I'm a student (m/f) _____	Sono uno studente/una studentessa
	Sono oono stoodayntay/oona
	stoodayntayssah
I am unemployed (m/f) _	Sono disoccupato/a
	Sono deesokkoopahto/ah
I'm retired _____	Sono pensionato/a
	Sono paynseeonahto/ah
I'm on a disability_____	Sono invalido/a al lavoro
pension	*Sono eenvahleedo/ah ahl lahvoro*
I'm a housewife _____	Sono casalinga
	Sono kahsahleengah
Do you like your job? _	Le/ti piace il Suo/tuo lavoro?
(formal/informal)	*Lay/tee peeahchay eel soo-o/too-o*
	lahvoro?
Most of the time_____	Per lo più sì
	Payr lo peeoo see
Mostly I do, but I prefer	Il più delle volte sì, però le vacanze mi
holidays	piacciono di più
	Eel peeoo dayllay voltay see, payro lay
	vahkahntzay mee peeahchono dee peeoo

3.3 Starting/ending a conversation

Could I ask you _____	Posso chiederLe/ti una cosa?
something?	*Posso keeaydayrlay/tee oonah kosah?*
(formal/informal)	
Excuse/Pardon me ____	Mi scusi/scusami
(formal/informal)	*Mee skoozee/skoozahmee*
Could you help me ____	Scusi, mi può aiutare?
please?	*Skoozee, mee pwo aheeootahray?*
Yes, what's the _____	Sì, che cosa c'è?
problem?	*See, kay kosah chay?*
What can I do for you? _	Di che cosa ha bisogno?
	Dee kay kosah ah beezoneeo?

Sorry, I don't have time now	**Mi dispiace, non ho tempo**
	Mee deespeeahchay, non o taympo
Do you have a light? (formal/informal)	**Ha/hai da accendere?**
	Ah/ay dah ahtchayndayhray?
May I join you?	**Posso farLe compagnia?**
	Posso fahrlay compahnee-ah?
Could you take a picture of me/us?	**Mi/ci potrebbe fare una foto?**
	Mee/chee potraybbay fahray oonah photo?
Leave me alone (formal/informal)	**Mi lasci/lasciami in pace**
	Mee lahshee/Lahshahmee een pahchay
Get lost (formal/informal)	**Se ne vada/Vattene**
	Say nay vahdah/Vahttenay
Go away or I'll scream	**Se non se ne va subito, strillo**
	Say non say nay vah soobeeto, streello

3.4 Congratulations and condolences

Happy birthday/many happy returns/happy name day	**Tanti auguri, buon compleanno/buon onomastico**
	Tahntee owgooree, bwon complayahnno/bwon onomahsteeko
Please accept my condolences.	**Le mie condoglianze**
	Lay meeay condollyahnzay
My deepest sympathy	**Mi dispiace moltissimo**
	Mee deespeeahchay molteesseemo

3.5 A chat about the weather

See also 1.5 The weather

It's so hot/cold today!	**Che caldo/freddo oggi!**
	Kay kahldo/frayddo odjee!
Isn't it a lovely day?	**Che bella giornata!**
	Kay bayllah jornahtah!

It's so windy/ _____ what a storm!	Che vento/temporale!
	Kay vaynto/taymporahlay!
All that rain/snow! _____	Che pioggia/neve!
	Kay peeodjah/nayhvay!
It's so foggy! _____	Che nebbia!
	Kay naybbeeah!
Has the weather been __ like this for long?	E' da parecchio che avete questo tempo?
	Ay dah pahraykkeeo kay ahvaytay kwaysto taympo?
Is it always this hot/ ___ cold here?	Fa sempre tanto caldo/freddo qui?
	Fah saympray tahnto kahldo/frayddo kwee?
Is it always this dry/____ humid here?	E' sempre tanto secco/umido qui?
	Ay saympray tahnto saykko/oomeedo kwee?

3.6 Hobbies

Do you have any _____ hobbies?(formal/ informal)	Ha/hai qualche hobby?
	Ah/ay kwahlkay obby?
I like knitting/_____ reading/photography/ DIY	Mi piace lavorare a maglia/leggere/la fotografia/il fai-da-te
	Mee peeahchay lahvoraray ah mahllyah/ledjayray/lah fotograhfeeah/eell fahee dah tay
I enjoy listening to _____ music	Mi piace ascoltare la musica
	Mee peeahchay ahskoltahray lah moozeekah
I play the guitar/the ___ piano	Suono la chitarra/il pianoforte
	Swono lah keetahrrah/eel peeahnofortay
I like the cinema_____	Mi piace andare al cinema
	Mee peeahchay ahndahray ahl cheenaymah

I like travelling/playing __   Mi piace viaggiare/fare dello sport/andare
   sport/going fishing/   a pesca/fare passeggiate
   going for a walk   *Mee peeahchay veeahdjahray/fahray dayllo*
       sport/ahndahray ah payskah/fahray
       pahssaydjahtay

3.7 Being the host(ess)

See also 4 Eating out

Can I offer you a drink?   Le/ti posso offrire qualcosa da bere?
   (formal/informal)   *Lay/tee posso offreeray kwahlkosah dah*
       bayray?
What would you like to _   Cosa beve?/Cosa bevi?
   drink? (formal/informal)   *Kozah bayvay?/Kozah bayvee?*
Something non- _____   Vorrei una bibita analcolica
   alcoholic, please.   *Vorrayèe oonah beebeetah ahnahlkoleekah*
Would you like a_____   Vuole una sigaretta/un sigaro?
   cigarette/cigar   *Vwolay oonah seegahrayttah/oon*
       seegahro?
I don't smoke _____   Non fumo
     Non foomo

3.8 Invitations

Are you doing anything _   Ha/hai qualcosa da fare stasera?
   tonight?   *Ah/ay kwahlkosah dah fahray stahsayhrah?*
   (formal/informal)
Do you have any plans _   Che intende/intendi fare oggi/questo
   for today/this   pomeriggio/stasera?
   afternoon/tonight?   *Kay eentaynday/eentayndee fahray*
   (formal/informal)   *odjee/kwaysto pomayreedjo/stahsayrah?*

Would you like to go ___ out with me? (formal/informal)	Le/ti piacerebbe uscire con me? *Lay/tee peeahchayraybbay oosheeray con may?*
Would you like to go ___ dancing with me? (formal/informal)	Le/ti piacerebbe andare a ballare con me? *Lay/tee peeahcherebbay ahndaray ah bahllahray con may?*
Would you like to have _ lunch/dinner with me? (formal/informal)	Le/ti piacerebbe venire a pranzo/a cena con me? *Lay/tee peeahchayraybbay vayneeray ah prahnzo/ah chaynah con may?*
Would you like to come to the beach with me? (formal/informal)	Le/ti piacerebbe venire alla spiaggia con me? *Lay/tee peeahchayraybbay vayneeray allah spee-ahdjah con may?*
Would you like to come into town with us? (formal/informal)	Le/ti piacerebbe venire in città con noi? *Lay/tee peeahchayraybbay vayneeray een cheettah con noee?*
Would you like to come and see some friends with us? (formal/informal)	Le/ti piacerebbe venire con noi a trovare degli amici? *Lay/tee peeahchayraybbay veneeray con noee ah trovahray daylly ahmeechee?*
Shall we dance?_____	Balliamo? *Bahlleeahmo?*
– sit at the bar? _____	Ci sediamo al bar? *Chee saydeeahmo ahl bahr?*
– get something to ___ drink?	Beviamo qualcosa? *Beveeahmo kwahlkosah?*
– go for a walk/drive? __	Vogliamo fare due passi? Facciamo un giro in macchina? *Vollyahmo fahray dooay pahssee? Fahtcheeahmo oon jeero een mahkkeenah?*
Yes, all right_____	Sí, va bene *See, vah baynay*
Good idea _____	E' una buona idea *Ay oonah bwonah eedayah*

44

No thank you	No grazie
	No, grahtzeeay
Maybe later	Più tardi, forse
	Peeoo tahrdy, forsay
I don't feel like it	Non mi va
	Non mee vah
I don't have time	Purtroppo non ho tempo
	Poortroppo non o taympo
I already have a date	Ho già un altro appuntamento
	O jah oonahltro ahppoontahmaynto
I'm not very good at dancing/volleyball/swimming	Non so ballare/giocare a pallavolo/nuotare
	Non so bahllahray/jokahray ah pahllahvolo/nwotahray

3.9 Paying a compliment

You look great! (formal/informal)	Sta/stai proprio bene!
	Stah/stahee propreeo bayhnay!
I like your car!	Che bella macchina!
	Kay bayllah mahkkeenah!
I like your ski outfit!	Che bel completo da sci!
	Kay bayl complayto dah shee!
You are very nice (formal/informal)	È/sei molto gentile
	Ay/say molto jaynteelay
What a good boy/girl!	Che bambino/a buono/a!
	Kay bahmbeeno/ah bwono/ah!
You're (formal) a good dancer	(Lei) balla molto bene
	(Layee) bahllah molto bayhnay
You're (formal) a very good cook	(Lei) cucina molto bene
	(Layee) koocheenah molto bayhnay
You're (formal) a good footballer	(Lei) sa giocare molto bene a calcio
	(Layee) sah jokahray molto bayhnay ah kahlcheeo

3.10 Chatting someone up

I like being with you____ Mi piace stare con te
Mee peeahchay stahray con tay

I've missed you _____ Mi sei mancato/a tanto
so much *Mee say mahnkahto/ah tahnto*

I dreamt about you ____ Ti ho sognato/a
(m/f) *Tee o sonyahto/ah*

I think about you all ___ Tutto il giorno penso a te
day *Tootto eel jorno paynso ah tay*

I've been thinking_____ Ho pensato a te tutto il giorno
about you all day *O paynsahto ah tay tootto eel jorno*

You have such a sweet _ Hai un bel sorriso
smile *Ahee oon bayl sorreezo*

You have such _____ I tuoi occhi sono bellissimi
beautiful eyes *Ee too-oee okkee sono baylleesseemee*

I love you (I'm fond ____ Ti voglio bene
of you) *Tee vollyo bayhnay*

I'm in love with _____ Sono innamorato/a di te
you (m/f) *Sono eennahmorahto/ah dee tay*

I'm in love with _____ Anch'io sono innamorato/a di te
you too (m/f) *Ankeeo sono eennahmorahto/ah dee tay*

I love you_____ Ti amo *Tee ahmo*

I love you too _____ Anch'io ti amo *Ahnkeeo tee ahmo*

I don't feel as strongly__ I miei sentimenti verso di te non sono
about you così intensi
Ee meeay saynteemayntee vayrso dee tay
non sono kozee eentaynsee

I already have a _____ Sono già fidanzato/a
girlfriend/boyfriend *Sono jah feedahntzahto/ah*

I'm not ready for that___ Me dispiace, non me la sento
Mee deespeeahchay, non may lah saynto

I don't want to rush ____ Non voglio precipitare le cose
into it *Non volleeo praycheepeetahray lay cosay*

Take your hands off ___ Non toccarmi
me *Non tokkahrmee*

Okay, no problem	O.k., non c'è problema
	O.K., non chay problaymah
Will you spend the night with me?	Rimani con me stanotte?
	Reemahnee con may stahnottay?
I'd like to go to bed with you	Vorrei andare a letto con te
	Vorrayee ahndahray ah laytto con tay
Only if we use a condom	Soltanto con un preservativo
	Solo kon oon praysayrvahteevo
We have to be careful about AIDS	Dobbiamo stare attenti a causa dell'aids
	Dobbyahmo stahray ahttayntee ah kaoosah dayll aheèids
That's what they all say	Questo lo dicono tutti
	Kwaysto lo deekono toottee
We shouldn't take any risks	Non possiamo correre rischi
	Non posseeahmo korrayray reeskee
Do you have a condom?	Hai un preservativo?
	Ahee oon praysayrvahteevo?
No? Then the answer's no	No? Allora lasciamo perdere
	No? Ahllorah lahshyahmo payrdayray

3.11 Arrangements

When will I see you again?	Quando La/ti rivedrò?
	Kwahndo lah/tee reevaydro?
Are you (informal) free over the weekend?	Sei libero/a al fine-settimana?
	Say leebayro/ah ahl feenay saytteemahnah?
What's the plan, then?	Come rimaniamo d'accordo?
	Komay reemahnyahmo dahkkordo?
Where shall we meet?	Dove ci vediamo?
	Dovay chee vaydyahmo?
Will you pick me/us up?	Mi/ci verrà a prendere?
	Mee/chee vayrrah ah prayndayray?
Shall I pick you (formal) up?	La passo a prendere?
	Lah pahsso ah prayndayray?

I have to be home by...	Devo essere a casa alle...
	Dayvo ayssayray ah cahsah ahllay...
I don't want to see ____ you (formal) anymore	Non voglio più rivederLa
	Non volleeo peeoo reevaydayrlah
Can I take you (formal) home?	Posso accompagnarLa a casa?
	Posso ahkkompahneeahrlah ah kahsah?

3.12 Saying goodbye

Can I write/call you (formal)?	Posso scriverLe/chiamarLa?
	Posso skreevayrlay/keeahmahrlah?
Will you (formal) write to me/call me?	Lei mi scriverà/chiamerà?
	Layeeh mee skreeverrah/keeahmaheerah?
Can I have your address/phone number?	Mi dà il Suo indirizzo/numero di telefono?
	Mee dah eel sooo eendeereetzo/ noomayro dee taylayfono?
Thanks for everything	Grazie di tutto
	Grahtzeeay dee tootto
It was a lot of fun	E' stato molto divertente
	Ay stahto molto deevayrtayntay
Say hello to (informal)...	Salutami... *Sahlootahmee...*
All the best	Tante belle cose
	Tahntay bayllay kosay
Good luck	Auguri *Owgooree*
When will you (informal) be back?	Quando tornerai?
	Kwahndo tornayrahee?
I'll be waiting for you (informal)	Ti aspetterò
	Tee ahspayttayrro
I'd like to see you again	Vorrei rivederti
	Vorrayee reevaydayrtee
I hope we meet again soon	Spero che ci rivedremo presto
	Spayro kay chee reevaydraymo praysto
Here's our address. If you're ever in England... (formal)	Ecco il nostro indirizzo. Casomai venisse in Inghilterra...
	Aykko eel nostro eendeereetzo. Kahzomahee vayneessay een Eengeelltayrrah

4 Eating out

● **Eating establishments:**

Trattoria: middle-price restaurant
Ristorante: prices vary but with better service than a *Trattoria*
Tavola calda: cheap, self-service style
Rosticceria: large selection of mainly take-away meals
Pizzeria: specialising in pizza
Osteria: small *trattoria* or wine bar
Gelateria: specialising in icecream
Bar/Caffè: café also serving alcohol and snack food
Birreria: bar specialising in beer

● **Mealtimes:**

In Italy people usually have three meals:
1 (*Prima*) *colazione* (breakfast), is eaten sometime between 7.30 and 10am, often standing up in a bar. It generally consists of *caffelatte* (white coffee) and biscuits or *cappuccino* with a *brioche* (croissant).
2 *Pranzo* (lunch), traditionally eaten at home between 1 and 2.30pm, includes a hot dish and is considered to be the most important meal of the day. Offices and shops often close and, unless enroled in a special afternoon programme, school children generally return home at lunchtime. Lunch usually consists of three courses:
- pasta or risotto
- main course of meat or fish with a vegetable or salad
- cheese and/or fruit
Antipasti (hors d'oeuvres preceding the pasta course), cakes and desserts are usually eaten on Sundays or on special occasions.
3 *Cena* (dinner), at around 8 or 9pm, is a light meal, often including soup, usually taken with the family.
At around 5pm, *merenda* (a snack) is often served to children and consists of bread and cured meats and/or cake.

● **In restaurants:** Most *trattorias* and restaurants have a cover charge (*coperto*) which includes bread, and a service charge.

4.1 On arrival

I'd like to book a table for seven o'clock, please	Vorrei prenotare un tavolo per le sette? *Vorrayee praynotahray oon tahvolo payr lay sayttay?*
A table for two, please	Un tavolo per due, per favore *Oon tahvolo payr dooay payr fahvoray*
We've (We haven't) booked	(Non) abbiamo prenotato *(Non) ahbbeeamo praynotahto*
Is the restaurant open yet?	Il ristorante è già aperto? *Eel reestorahntay ay jah ahpayrto?*
What time does the restaurant open?/What time does the restaurant close?	A che ora apre il ristorante/A che ora chiude il ristorante? *Ah kay orah ahpray eel reestorahntay?/Ah kay orah keeooday eel reestorahntay?*
Can we wait for a table?	Possiamo aspettare che si liberi un tavolo? *Possyahmo ahspayttahray kay see leebayree oon tahvolo?*
Do we have to wait long?	Dobbiamo aspettare parecchio? *Dobbyahmo ahspayttahray pahraykkeeo?*
Is this seat taken?	E' libero questo posto? *Ay leebayro kwaysto posto?*

Ha prenotato?	Do you have a reservation?
A che nome?	What name, please?
Prego, da questa parte	This way, please
Questo tavolo è prenotato	This table is reserved
Fra un quarto d'ora ci sarà un tavolo libero	We'll have a table free in fifteen minutes.
Le dispiace aspettare nel frattempo?	Would you mind waiting?

Could we sit _____ here/there?	Possiamo accomodarci qui/lì?
	Possyahmo ahkkomodahrchee kwee/lee?
Can we sit by the_____ window?	Possiamo sedere vicino alla finestra?
	Possyahmo sayhdayray veecheeno ahllah feenaystrah?
Are there any tables____ outside?	Si può mangiare anche fuori?
	See pwo mahnjahray ahnkay fworee?
Do you have another ___ chair for us?	Ha un'altra sedia?
	Ah oonahltrah saydyah?
Do you have a _____ highchair?	Ha un seggiolone (per bambini)?
	Ah oon saydjolonay (payr bahmbeenee)?
Is there a socket for____ this bottle-warmer?	C'è una presa di corrente per lo scaldabiberon?
	Chay oonah praysah dee corrayntay payr lo skahldahbeebayron?
Could you warm up ____ this bottle/jar for me? (in the microwave)	Potrebbe riscaldare questo biberon/vasetto (nel forno a microonde)?
	Potraybbay reeskahldahray kwaysto beebayron/vahzaytto (nayl forno ah meekroonday)?
Not too hot, please ____	Non bollente, per favore
	Non bollayntay payr fahvoray
Is there somewhere I ___ can change the baby's nappy?	C'è un posto dove posso cambiare il bambino/la bambina?
	Chay oon posto dovay posso kahmbeeahray eel bahmbeeno/lah bahmbeenah?
Where are the toilets? __	Dove è il bagno?
	Dovay ay eel bahnyo?

4.2 Ordering

| Waiter/Waitress! _____ | Cameriere/a! |
| | *Kahmayreeayray/ah!* |

Madam! _____	Signora! *Seeneeeorah!*
Sir!_____	Signore! *Seeneeeoray!*
We'd like something to _ eat/drink	Vorremmo mangiare/bere qualcosa *Vorraymmo mahnjahray/bayhray kwahlkosah*
Could I have a quick ___ meal?	Potrei mangiare qualcosa rapidamente? *Potray mahnjahray kwahlkosah rahpeedahmayntay?*
We don't have much ___ time	Abbiamo poco tempo *Ahbbeeahmo poko taympo*
We'd like to have a ____ drink first	Vorremmo prima bere qualcosa *Vorraymmo preemah bayhray kwahlkosah*
Could we see the_____ menu/wine list, please?	Ci porta il menù/la lista dei vini, per favore? *Chee portah eel maynoo/lah leestah dayee veenee payr fahvoray?*
Do you have a menu ___ in English?	Ha un menù in inglese? *Ah oon maynoo een eenglaysay?*
Do you have a dish of _ the day/a tourist menu?	Ha un piatto del giorno/un menù turistico? *Ah oon peeahtto dayl jorno/oon maynoo tooreesteeko?*

Desidera?	What would you like?
Ha scelto?	Have you decided?
Vuole un aperitivo?	Would you like a drink first?
Cosa prende da bere?	What would you like to drink?
... sono finiti/e	We've run out of.....
Buon appetito	Enjoy your meal/Bon appetit
Tutto bene?	Is everything all right?
Posso sparecchiare?	May I clear the table?

English	Italian
We haven't made a ___ choice yet.	Non abbiamo ancora deciso *Non ahbbeeahmo ahnkorah daycheezo*
What do you ___ recommend?	Cosa ci consiglia? *Kosah chee konseellyah?*
What are the local ___ specialities/your specialities?	Quali sono le specialità di questa regione/della casa? *Kwahlee sono lay spaycheeahleetah dee kwaystah rayjonay/dayllah kahsah?*
I like strawberries/ olives	Mi piacciono le fragole/le olive *Mee peeahtchono lay frahgolay/lay oleevay*
I don't like meat/fish...___	Non mi piace il pesce/la carne *Non mee peeahchay eel payshay/lah kahrnay*
What's this? ___	Cosa è questo? *Kosah ay kwaysto?*
Does it have...in it? ___	Contiene...? *Konteeayhnay...?*
Is it stuffed with...? ___	E' farcito di...? *Ay fahrcheeto dee...?*
What does it taste like?	Che sapore ha? *Kay sahporay ah?*
Is this a hot or a ___ cold dish?	E' un piatto caldo o freddo? *Ay oon peeahtto kahldo o frayddo?*
Is this sweet? ___	E' dolce? *Ay dolchay?*
Is this hot/spicy? ___	E' un piatto piccante/aromatizzato? *Ay oon peeahtto peekkahntay/ahromahteedzahto?*
Do you have anything ___ else, by any chance?	Avrebbe magari qualcos'altro? *Ahvraybbay mahgahree kwahlkosahltro?*
I'm on a salt-free diet ___	Non posso mangiare sale *Non posso mahnjahray sahlay*
I can't eat pork ___	Non posso mangiare carne di maiale *Non posso mahnjahray kahrnay dee maheeahlay*
I can't have sugar ___	Non posso mangiare zuccheri *Non posso mahnjahray dzookkayree*

I'm on a fat-free diet ___	**Non posso mangiare grassi**
	Non posso mahnjahray grahssee
I can't have spicy food _	**Non posso mangiare cibi piccanti**
	Non posso mahnjahray cheebee peekkahntee
We'll have what those __ people are having	**Vorremmo un piatto uguale al loro**
	Vorraymmo oon peeahtto oogwahlay ahl loro
I'd like... _____	**Vorrei...**
	Vorrayee...
We're not having _____ antipasto/a pasta dish	**Passiamo subito al primo/secondo piatto**
	Pahsseeahmo soobeeto ahl preemo/saykondo peeahtto
Could I have some____ more bread, please?	**Mi porta un altro po' di pane, per favore?**
	Mee portah oonahltro po dee pahnay payr fahvoray?
Could I have another ___ bottle of water/wine, please?	**Mi porta un'altra bottiglia di acqua/di vino, per favore?**
	Mee portah oonahltrah botteelleeah dee ahkwah/dee veeno payr fahvoray?
Could I have another____ portion of... please?	**Mi porta un'altra porzione di..., per favore?**
	Mee portah oonahltrah portzeeonay dee..., payr fahvoray?
Could I have the salt ___ and pepper, please?	**Mi porta il sale e il pepe, per favore?**
	Mee portah eel sahlay ay eel paypay, payr fahvoray?
Could I have a napkin, _ please?	**Mi porta un tovagliolo, per favore?**
	Mee portah oon tovallyolo, payr fahvoray?
Could I have a _____ teaspoon, please?	**Mi porta un cucchiaino, per favore?**
	Mee portah oon kookkeeaheeno payr fahvoray?
Could I have an _____ ashtray, please?	**Mi porta un portacenere, per favore?**
	Mee portah oon portahchaynayray, payr fahvoray?
Could I have some____ matches, please?	**Mi porta dei fiammiferi, per favore?**
	Mee portah dayee feeahmmeefayree payr fahvoray?

Could I have some_____ toothpicks, please	Mi porta degli stuzzicadenti, per favore?
	Mee portah daylly stootzeekahdayntee payr fahvoray?
Could I have a glass of _ water, please?	Mi porta un bicchiere d'acqua, per favore?
	Mee portah oon beekkeeayray dahkwah payr fahvoray?
Could I have a straw __ please?	Mi porta una cannuccia, per favore?
	Mee portah oonah kahnnootchah payr fahvoray?
Enjoy your meal/Bon ___ appetit!	Buon appetito!
	Bwon ahppayteeto!
You too! _____	Grazie, altrettanto!
	Grahtzeeay, ahltrayttahnto!
Cheers!_____	Cin cin!
	Cheen cheen!
The next round's on me	La prossima volta offro io
	Lah prosseemah voltah offro eeo
Could we have a doggy bag, please?	Potremmo portare via gli avanzi per il nostro cane?
	Potraymmo portahray veeah lly ahvahntzee payr eel nostro kahnay?

4.3 The bill

See also 8.2 Settling the bill

How much is this dish?	Quanto costa questo piatto?
	Kwahnto kostah kwaysto peeahtto?
Could I have the bill, ___ please?	Ci porti il conto
	Chee portee eel konto
All together _____	Tutto insieme
	Tootto eensee-aymay
Everyone pays _____ separately/ let's go Dutch	Facciamo alla romana
	Fahtcheeahmo ahllah romahnah

Could we have the ____ menu again, please?	Ci porta di nuovo il menu?
	Chee portah dee nwovo eel maynoo?
The...is not on the bill ___	Ha dimenticato di mettere il/la... sul conto
	Ah deemaynteekahto dee mayttayray eel/lah...sool konto

4.4 Complaints

It's taking a very _____ long time	C'è ancora molto da aspettare?
	Chay ahnkorah molto dah ahspayttahray?
We've been here an ____ hour already	E' un'ora che stiamo qui
	Ay oonorah kay steeahmo kwee
This must be a mistake_	Senz'altro è uno sbaglio
	Saynzahltro ay oono sbahleeo
This is not what I _____ ordered	Non ho ordinato questo piatto
	Non o ordeenahto kwaysto peeahtto
I ordered... _____	Ho chiesto...
	O keeaysto...
There's a dish missing_	Manca un piatto
	Mahnkah oon peeahtto
This is broken/not _____ clean	Questo è rotto/non è pulito
	Kwaysto ay rotto/non ay pooleeto
The food's cold_____	Il piatto è freddo
	Eel peeahtto ay frayddo
The food's not fresh ___	Il cibo non è fresco
	Eel cheebo non ay fraysko
The food's too salty/ ___ sweet/spicy	Il piatto è troppo salato/dolce/ aromatizzato
	Eel peeahtto ay troppo sahlahto/dolchay/ahromahteedzahto
The meat's too rare ____	La carne è poco cotta
	Lah kahrnay ay poko kottah
The meat's overdone___	La carne è troppo cotta
	Lah kahrnay ay troppo kottah

The meat's tough _____	La carne è dura
	Lah kahrnay ay doorah
The meat is off/has ____ gone bad	La carne è andata a male
	Lah kahrnay ay ahndahtah ah mahlay
Could I have _____ something else instead of this?	Invece di questo, mi potrebbe dare un'altra cosa?
	Eenvayhchay dee kwaysto mee potraybbay dahray oonahltrah kosah?
The bill/this amount is _ not right	Il conto non torna
	Eel konto non tornah
We didn't have this ____	Non abbiamo preso questo
	Non ahbbeeahmo prayso kwaysto
There's no paper in the _ toilet	Manca la carta igienica nel bagno
	Mahnkah lah kahrtah eejayneekah nayl bahneeo
Will you call the _____ manager, please?	Mi chiama il capo-servizio, per favore?
	Mee keeahmah eel kahpo-sayrveetzeeo payr fahvoray?

4.5 Paying a compliment

That was a wonderful __ meal	Abbiamo mangiato molto bene
	Ahbbeeahmo mahnjahto molto bayhnay
The food was excellent _	Il cibo era ottimo
	Eel cheebo ayrah otteemo
The...in particular was __ delicious	Soprattutto... era squisito/a
	Soprahttootto...ayrah skweezeeto/ah

4.6 The menu

antipasti starter/hors
 d'oeuvres
cacciagione game
carne meat
contorni side
 dishes/vegetables
coperto cover charge
digestivo liqueur
 (after dinner)
dolci cakes/desserts
formaggio cheese

frutta fruit
gelati icecream
insalata salad
I.V.A. VAT
minestra soup
pane bread
pasta (sciutta)
 pasta
pesce fish
pizzapizza
pollame fowl

primo piatto first
 course
secondo piatto main
 course
servizio (compreso)
 service charge
 (included)
specialità specialities
spuntini snacks
verdure vegetables

4.7 Alphabetical list of drinks and dishes

acciuga
anchovy
acqua (minerale)
(mineral) water
affettati
sliced cured
 meats
affumicato
smoked
aglio
garlic
agnello
lamb
amatriciana, all'
(with) bacon, chilli
 and tomato sauce
 (for pasta)

anatra duck
anguilla (carpionata)
eel (soused)
aranciata
orange juice/ade
arista
roast pork
arrabbiata, all'
(with) chilli and
 tomato sauce (for
 pasta)
arrosto
roast
asparago
asparagus
bianco (in)
without seasoning

birra
beer
bistecca
steak
bollito
boiled meat
braciola
minute steak
brasato
braised
brodo
broth
bruschetta
toasted bread with
 garlic topping
budino
pudding

burro
butter
cacciatora, alla
(with) mushroom
sauce (esp. for
chicken)
caffè corretto/
macchiato
laced or flavoured
coffee/coffee with a
drop of milk
caffè freddo
iced coffee
caffè (lungo/ristretto)
coffee (weak/strong)
caffellatte
Café au lait/milky
coffee
calamaro squid
cannelloni
cannelloni (pasta
tubes)
cappero
caper
cappuccino
cappuccino (coffee
with frothy milk)
carbonara, alla
(with) cream, bacon,
egg, black pepper
and parmesan
sauce (for pasta)
carciofo
artichoke
carota
carrot

carpa
carp
carrettiera, alla
(with) tomato, garlic,
chilli and parsley
sauce (for pasta)
casalingo
home-made
cassata
cassata (Sicilian
fruited icecream)
cavolfiore
cauliflower
cavolini di Bruxelles
Brussels sprouts
cavolo
cabbage
ceci
chick peas
cervello
brains
cervo
venison
cetriolino
gherkin
cetriolo
cucumber
cicoria
chicory
cinghiale
boar
cioccolata
chocolate
cipolla onion
coda di bue
oxtail

condito
dressed
coniglio
rabbit
coscia
leg (of chicken, of
lamb)
cotoletta
cutlet
cozze
mussels
crema
custard
crostini
canapé with savoury
topping/croutons
crudo
raw
digestivo
liqueur (after dinner)
erbe aromatiche
herbs
fagiano
pheasant
fagioli
beans
fagiolini
green beans
faraona
guinea fowl
farcito
stuffed
fegato
liver
alla brace
barbequed/grilled

fetta/fettina	gran(o)turco	marinato
slice/thin slice	corn	marinated/pickled
filetto	grappa	melanzana
fillet	eau de vie	eggplant/aubergine
finocchio	griglia, alla	merluzzo
fennel	grilled	cod
forno, al	imbottito	miele
baked	stuffed	honey
frappé	infuso	minestrone
milk-shake	infusion (tea)	minestrone soup
frittata	intingolo di lepre	molluschi
omelette	hare sauce	shellfish
fritto fried	involtino	noce
frizzante	roulade	walnut
fizzy	latte	noce moscata
frullato	milk	nutmeg
milk-shake/whisked	lepre	olio
frutti di mare	hare	oil
seafood	limone (al)	oliva
funghi	(with) lemon	olive
mushrooms	lingua	ossobuco
gamberetto	tongue	veal shin
shrimp	liquore	ostrica
gambero	liqueur	oyster
crayfish	lombata/lombo	pancetta
gelato	loin	bacon
icecream	luccio	pane
ghiaccio (con)	pike	(integrale/tostato)
(with) ice	lumache	bread (wholemeal/
giardiniera, alla	snails	toasted)
(with) vegetable	maccheroni	panino (imbottito)
sauce	macaroni (pasta)	bread-roll (filled)
gnocchi	macedonia di frutta	panna (montata)
potato dumplings	fruit salad	(whipped) cream
granchio	manzo	parmigiano
crab	beef	parmesan (cheese)

passata sieved or creamed

pasta pasta

pastasciutta pasta (with sauce)

pasta sfoglia puff pastry

pasticcio (sort of) pie (often made of pasta)

patate fritte chips

pecora sheep/mutton

pecorino sheep's milk cheese

penne pasta quills

peperoncino chilli

peperone (green, red, yellow) pepper

pesto basil, pine-nut and parmesan sauce

petto breast

piccione pigeon

piselli peas

pizzaiola, alla (with) mozzarella cheese, oregano and tomato sauce

pollo chicken

polpetta meatball

pomodoro tomato

porchetta suckling pig

porcini (porcini) mushrooms

porto Port (wine)

prezzemolo parsley

prosciutto cured ham

puttanesca, alla (with) spicy tomato sauce

quaglia quail

rapa turnip

ragù meat (Bolognese) sauce

riccio di mare sea urchin

rigatoni rigatoni (large pasta tubes)

ripieno stuffed

riso rice

risotto risotto

rognone kidney

rosbiff roast beef

salame salami

salmone salmon

salsa sauce

salsiccia sausage

saltimbocca veal with prosciutto and sage

salumi cured meats

sambuca sweet aniseed liqueur

sarda, sardina sardine

scaloppina escalope

scampi prawns

secco dry

sedano celery

sel(t)z soda water

selvaggina game

semifreddo icecream cake

senape
mustard

seppia
cuttle fish

sogliola
sole

sottaceti
pickles

spalla
shoulder

spezzatino
stew

spiedo, allo
on the spit

spina, alla
draught (beer)

spinaci
spinach

spremuta
(freshly squeezed)
juice

spumante
sparkling wine

S.Q. secondo
quantità
according to
weight

stracciatella
soup: broth with
beaten egg

stufato
stew

succo di frutta
fruit juice

sugo
sauce

tacchino
turkey

tagliatelle
tagliatelle (flat ribbon
pasta)

tartaruga
turtle

tartufo
truffle

tè
tea

testa (di vitello)
head (of veal)

tonno tuna

torta
pie/cake

tortellini
tortellini (kind of
stuffed pasta)

trippa
tripe

trita(ta)
minced or ground
(usually herbs or
meat)

trota
trout

uova strapazzate
scrambled eggs

uovo affogato/in
camicia
poached egg

uovo al tegame/fritto
fried egg

uovo, all'
(with) egg

uovo alla coque/da
bere/sodo
soft boiled/fresh/hard
boiled egg

vaniglia
vanilla

verdura
green vegetables

vino bianco/rosso/
rosato
white/red/rosé wine

vitello
veal

vongola
clam

zabaione
zabaglione (sweet
custard sauce made
with egg and
Marsala)

zucchero
sugar

zucchino
courgette (small
marrow, squash)

zuppa
soup

zuppa alla pavese
kind of broth

zuppa inglese
kind of trifle

5

On the road

5.1 Asking for directions

Excuse me, could I ask you something?	Mi scusi, potrei chiederLe una cosa?
	Mee skoozee potray keeaydayrlay oonah kozah?
I've lost my way _____	Mi sono perso/a
	Mee sono payrso/ah
Is there a(n)... _____ around here?	Sa se c'è un/una... da queste parti?
	Sah say chay oon/oonah...dah kwaystay pahrtee?
Is this the way to...? ___	E' questa la strada per...?
	Ay kwaystah lah strahdah payr...
Could you tell me how to get to....?	Mi può indicare la strada per...?
	Mee pwo eendeekahray lah strahdah payr...
What's the quickest way to...?	Qual'è la strada più diretta per...?
	Kwahlay ay lah strahdah peeoo deerayttah payr...?
How many kilometres is it to...?	A quanti chilometri è...?
	Ah qwahntee keelomaytreeay....?
Could you point it out on the map?	Me lo può indicare sulla mappa?
	May lo pwo eendeekahray soollah mahppah?

Vada dritto	la strada	il fiume
Go straight ahead	the road/street	the river
Giri a sinistra	il semaforo	il viadotto
Turn left	the traffic light	the flyover
Giri a destra	la galleria the tunnel	il ponte
Turn right	il cartello/segnale	the bridge
Volti a destra/sinistra	stradale di 'dare la	il passaggio a livello
Turn right/left	precedenza'	the level crossing
Segua Follow	the "give way" sign	le indicazioni per...
Attraversi Cross	il palazzo	the signs pointing
l'incrocio	the building	to....
the intersection/	all'angolo	la freccia
crossroads	at the corner	the arrow

Non lo so, non sono di questa città/regione	I don't know, I don't know my way around here
Ha sbagliato strada	You're going the wrong way
Deve ritornare a...	You have to go back to...
Là, deve seguire le indicazioni	From there on just follow the signs
Là, chieda di nuovo	When you get there, ask again

5.2 Customs

By law you must always carry with you an identification document and, if driving, your driving licence.

● **Border documents:** valid passport. Citizens of EU countries may enter Italy using a national identity card. Strictly speaking, visitors planning to stay at the same address for more than one week need a *permesso di soggiorno*, obtained from the *questura* (police station) and requiring a visa stamp. This only becomes a necessity if you plan to study, work or live in Italy.

Il passaporto, prego	Your passport, please
La carta verde, prego	Your green card, please
Il libretto d'immatricolazione, prego	Your vehicle documents, please
Il visto, prego	Your visa, please
Dove va?	Where are you going?
Quanto tempo intende rimanere?	How long are you planning to stay?
Ha qualcosa da dichiarare?	Do you have anything to declare?
Per favore, mi apra questo/a	Open this, please

● **For car and motorbike:** valid full driving licence, together with paper counterpart if photocard licence (older licences may be accompanied by an International Driving Permit), vehicle registration document and motor insurance certificate. Contact your motor insurer for advice at least a month before taking your vehicle overseas to ensure that you are adequately covered.

● **Caravan:** same registration numberplate.

It is compulsory for the driver and/or passenger(s) to wear a reflective jacket/waistcoat when exiting a vehicle which is immobilised on the carriageway of all motorways and main or busy roads. A warning triangle is compulsory (bulb kit, fire extinguisher and first-aid kit are recommended).

● **Import and export restrictions:**

Within the European Union travellers are only subject to selective spot checks. There is no restriction, either by quantity or value, on goods purchased in another EU country provided they are for personal use. Visitors from other countries are advised to contact a travel agent, customs, or the Embassy before travelling.

My children are _____ entered on this passport	I miei figli sono su questo passaporto *Ee meeayee feelly sono soo kwaysto pahssahporto*
I'm travelling through___	Sono di passaggio *Sono dee pahssahdjo*
I'm going on holiday ___ to...	Passerò le vacanze a... *Pahssayhro lay vahkahntzay ah...*
I'm on a business trip ___	Sono in viaggio d'affari *Sono een veeahdjo dahffahree*
I don't know how long ___ I'll be staying	Non so quanto tempo rimarrò *Non so kwahnto taympo reemahrro*
I'll be staying here for ___ a weekend	Rimarrò qui un weekend *Reemahrro kwee oon weekend*
I'll be staying here for ___ a few days	Rimarrò qui qualche giorno *Reemahrro kwee kwahlkay jorno*
I'll be staying here _____ a week	Rimarrò qui una settimana *Reemahrro kwee oonah saytteemahnah*

I'll be staying here for two weeks	Rimarrò qui due settimane
	Reemahrro kwee dooay saytteemahnay
I've got nothing to declare	Non ho niente da dichiarare
	Non o neeayntay dah deekeeeahrahray
I have...	Ho...
	O...
– a carton of cigarettes	– una stecca di sigarette
	– oonah staykkah dee seegahrayttay
– a bottle of...	– una bottiglia di...
	– oonah botteellyah dee...
– some souvenirs	– qualche souvenir
	– kwahlkay sovayneer
These are personal effects	Sono oggetti personali
	Sono odjayttee payrsonahlee
These are not new	Questa roba non è nuova
	Kwaystah robah non ay nwovah
Here's the receipt	Ecco lo scontrino
	Aykko lo skontreeno
This is for private use	E' per uso personale
	Ay payr oozo payrsonahlay
How much import duty do I have to pay?	Quanto devo pagare di tassa d'importazione?
	Kwahnto dayvo pahgahray dee tahssah deemportahtzeeonay ?
May I go now?	Posso andare adesso?
	Posso ahndahray ahdaysso?

5.3 Luggage

Porter!	Facchino!
	Fahkkeeno!
Could you take this luggage to...?	Per favore, potrebbe portare questi bagagli a...
	Payr fahvoray, potraybbay portahray kwaystee bahgahlly ah...

How much do I owe you?	Quanto Le devo?
	Kwahnto lay dayvo?
Where can I find a trolley?	Dove posso trovare un carrello?
	Dovay posso trovahray oon kahrrello?
Could you store this luggage for me?	E' possibile lasciare in consegna questi bagagli?
	Ay posseebeelay lahsheeahray een konsayneeah kwaystee bahgahlly?
Where are the luggage lockers?	Dove sono le cassette per la custodia dei bagagli?
	Dovay sono lay kahssayttay payr lah koostodeeah dayee bahgahlly?
I can't get the locker open	Non riesco ad aprire la cassetta
	Non ree-aysko ahdahpreeray lah kahssaytta
How much is it per item per day?	Quanto costa al giorno ogni collo?
	Kwahnto kostah ahl jorno onyee kollo?
This is not my bag/suitcase	Non è la mia borsa/valigia
	Non ay lah meeah borsah/vahleejah
There's one item/bag/suitcase missing	Manca un collo/una borsa/una valigia
	Mahnkah oon kollo/oonah borsah/oonah vahleejah
My suitcase is damaged	La mia valigia è danneggiata
	Lah meeah vahleejah ay dahnnaydjahtah

5.4 Traffic signs

accendere i fari (in galleria) switch on headlights (in the tunnel)	attenzione beware	caduta massi beware, falling rocks
alt stop	autocarri heavy goods vehicles	cambiare corsia change lanes
area/stazione di servizio service station	banchina non transitabile impassable verge	chiuso al traffico road closed corsia di emergenza emergency lane

curve
bends
deviazione
detour
disco orario
(obbligatorio)
parking disk
(compulsory)
divieto di accesso
no entry
divieto di
sorpasso/di sosta
no overtaking/no
parking
diritto di
precedenza a fine
strada
right of way at end of
road
galleria tunnel
incrocio
intersection/
crossroads
(isola/zona)
pedonale
traffic island/
pedestrian
precinct
lasciare libero il
passo/passaggio
do not obstruct
lavori in corso
roadworks
pagamento/
pedaggio
toll payment

parcheggio a
pagamento/
riservato a...
paying
carpark/parking
reserved for...
parcheggio
custodito
supervised carpark
passaggio a livello
level crossing
altezza limitata a...
maximum head
room...
passo carrabile
driveway
pericolo(so)
danger(ous)
pioggia o gelo per
km....
rain or ice for...kms
precedenza
right of way
rallentare
slow down
senso unico
one way
senso vietato
no entry
soccorso stradale
road assistance
(breakdown
service)
sosta limitata
parking for a limited
period

strada deformata/in
dissesto
broken/uneven
surface
strada interrotta
road closed
strettoia
narrowing in the road
tenere la
destra/sinistra
keep right/left
traffico interrotto
road blocked
transito con catene
snow-chains required
uscita
exit
velocità massima
maximum speed
vietato l'accesso/ai
pedoni
no access/no
pedestrian access
vietato l'autostop
no hitch-hiking
vietato svoltare a
destra/sinistra
no right/left turn
zona disco
disk zone
zona rimozione
(ambo i lati)
tow-away area (both
sides of the road)

5.5 The car

● **Particular traffic regulations:**
Speed limits: on *autostradas* 130km/h for cars of 1100cc or more;
110km/h for smaller cars and motorbikes under 350cc.
On all main, non-urban highways 110km/h; on secondary, non-urban
highways 90km/h; in built-up areas 50km/h.
Give way to vehicles coming from the right unless otherwise
indicated.
– towing: prohibited to private drivers.

5.6 The petrol station

● **Petrol stations** keep shop hours, though they may be open later
in the evening. Even motorway petrol stations close at night. Very
few take credit cards, except on the *autostradas*.

How many kilometres to the next petrol station, please?	A quanti chilometri sta il prossimo distributore di benzina?
	Ah kwahntee keelomaytree sta eel prossemo deestreebootoray dee baynzeenah?
I would like...litres of	Vorrei... litri di
	Vorrayee... leetree dee
– super	Vorrei... litri di super
	Vorrayee... leetree dee soopayr
– leaded	Vorrei... litri di normale
	Vorrayee... leetree dee normahlay
– unleaded	Vorrei... litri di benzina senza piombo
	Vorrayee... leetree dee baynzeenah saynzah peeombo
– diesel	Vorrei... litri di gasolio
	Vorrayee... leetree dee gahzoleeo

The parts of a car

battery	batteria	*bahttayreeyah*
rear light	il fanale posteriore	*eel fahnahlay postayry-oray*
rear-view mirror	lo specchietto retrovisore	*lo spaykkeeaytto raytroveezoray*
reversing light	la luce di retromarcia	*lah loochay dee raytromahrcheeah*
aerial	antenna	*ahntaynnah*
car radio	autoradio (f)	*ahootorahdeeo*
petrol tank	serbatoio carburante	*sayrbahtoeeo kahrboorahntay*
sparking plugs	le candele	*lay kahndaylay*
fuel pump	pompa della benzina	*pompah dayllah bayndzeenah*
wing mirror	lo specchietto retrovisore esterno	*lo spaykkeeaytto raytroveezoray aystayrno*
bumper	il paraurti	*eel pahrah-oortee*
carburettor	il carburatore	*eel kahrboorahtoray*
crankcase	basamento del motore	*bahsahmaynto dayl motoray*
cylinder	cilindro	*cheeleendro*
ignition	accensione (f)	*ahtchaynseeonay*
warning light	spia luminosa	*spee-ah loomeenohzah*
dynamo	la dinamo	*lah deenahmo*
accelerator	acceleratore (m)	*ahtchayllayrahtoray*
handbrake	freno a mano	*frayno ah mahno*
valve	valvola	*vahlvolah*
silencer	marmitta	*mahrmeettah*
boot	cofano	*kofahno*
headlight	faro	*fahro*
crank shaft	albero a gomiti	*ahlbayro ah gomeetee*
air filter	filtro dell'aria	*feeltro dayllahreea*
fog lamp	faro fendinebbia	*fahro fayndeenaybbeeah*
engine block	monoblocco	*monoblokko*

camshaft	albero a camme	*ahlbayro ah kahmmay*
oil filter/pump	filtro/pompa dell'olio	*feeltro/pompah daylloleeo*
dipstick	indicatore (m) di livello dell'olio	*eendeekahtoray dee leevayllo daylloleeo*
pedal	il pedale	*eel paydahlay*
door	portiera	*porteeayrah*
radiator	il radiatore	*eel rahdeeahtoray*
brake disc	disco del freno	*deesko dayl frayno*
spare wheel	ruota di scorta	*rwohtah dee skortah*
indicator	indicatore (m) (di direzione)	*eendeekahtoray (dee deeraytzeeonay)*
windscreen wiper	tergicristallo	*tayrjeekreestahllo*
shock absorbers	ammortizzatore (m)	*ahmmorteedzahtoray*
sunroof	tetto apribile	*taytto ahpreebeelay*
spoiler	lo spoiler	*lo spoeelayr*
starter motor	motorino di avviamento	*motoreeno dee ahvveeahmaynto*
steering column	il piantone dello sterzo	*eel peeahntonay dayllo stayrtzo*
steering wheel	il volante	*eel volahntay*
exhaust pipe	tubo di scarico	*toobo dee skahreeko*
seat belt	cintura di sicurezza	*cheentoorah dee seekooraytzah*
fan	il ventilatore	*eel vaynteelahtoray*
distributor cables	i cavi del distributore	*ee kahvee dayl deestreebootoray*
gear lever	leva del cambio	*layvah del kahmbeeo*
windscreen	il parabrezza	*eel pahrahbrayzah*
water pump	pompa dell'acqua	*pompah dayllahkkwah*
wheel	ruota	*rwotah*
hubcap	coprimozzo	*kopreemotzo*
piston	il pistone	*eel peestonay*

The parts of a bicycle

rear lamp	fanalino posteriore	*fahnahleeno postayreeoray*
rear wheel	ruota posteriore	*rwotah postayreeoray*
(luggage) carrier	il portapacchi	*eel portahpahkkee*
fork	forcella	*forchayllah*
bell	campanello	*kahmpahnayllo*
inner tube	camera d'aria	*kahmayrah dahreeyah*
tyre	gomma	*gommah*
peddle crank	pedivella	*payhdeevayllah*
gear change	cambio	*kahmbeeo*
wire	filo	*feelo*
dynamo	la dinamo	*lah deenahmo*
bicycle trailer	carrello	*kahrrayllo*
frame	telaio	*tayllahee-oh*
wheel guard	il pararuota	*eel pahrah-rwohtah*
chain	catena	*kahtaynah*
chain guard	il copricatena	*eel kopreekahtaynah*
odometer	il contachilometri	*eel kontahkeelomayhtree*
child's seat	il seggiolino	*eel saydjholeeno*
headlamp	il fanale	*eel fahnahlay*
bulb	lampadina	*lahmpahdeenah*
pedal	il pedale	*eel paydahlay*
pump	pompa	*pompah*

... euro worth of gas ___	Vorrei... euro di benzina
	Vorrayee... euro dee baynzeenah
Fill her up, please ____	Mi faccia il pieno per favore
	Mee fahtchah eel peeayno payr fahvoray
Could you check...? ___	Può controllarmi...?
	Pwo controllahrmee...?
– the oil level _____	– il livello dell'olio
	– eel leevayllo daylloleeo
– the tyre pressure ____	– la pressione delle gomme
	– lah praysseeonay dayllay gommay

reflector	il catarifrangente	*eel kahtahreefrahndjayhntay*
brake pad	pastiglia	*pahsteelleeah*
brake cable	cavo del freno	*kahvo dayl frayno*
anti-theft device	antifurto (m)	*ahnteefoorto*
carrier straps	le cinghie del portapacchi	*lay cheengeeay dayl portahpahkkee*
tachometer	tachimetro	*tahkeemaytro*
spoke	raggio	*rahjeeo*
mudguard	parafango	*pahrahfahngo*
handlebar	manubrio	*mahnoobreeo*
chain wheel	ruota dentata	*rwotah dayntahtah*
toe clip	il fermapiede	*eel fayrmahpeeayday*
crank axle	albero delle pedivelle	*ahlbayro dayllay paydeevayllay*
drum brake	freno a tamburo	*frayno ah tahmbooro*
rim	il cerchione	*eel chayrkeeoonay*
valve	valvola	*vahlvolah*
gear cable	cavo del cambio	*kahvo dayl kahmbeeo*
fork	forcella	*forchayllah*
front wheel	ruota anteriore	*rwotah ahntayreeooray*
seat	sellino (sella)	*saylleeno (sayllah)*

Could you change the _ oil, please?	Può cambiarmi l'olio?	
	Pwo kahmbeeahrmeo loleeo?	
Could you clean the ___ windscreen, please?	Può lavarmi il parabrezza?	
	Pwo lahvahrmeo eel pahrahbraydzah?	
Could you give the car_ a wash, please?	Può lavarmi la macchina?	
	Pwo lahvahrmee lah mahkkeenah?	

5.7 Breakdown and repairs

I have broken down____ Could you give me a hand?	Sono rimasto/a in panne. Mi potrebbe dare una mano? *Sono reaymahsto/ah een pahnnay. Mee potraybbay dahray oonah mahno?*
I (m/f) have run out of ___ petrol	Sono rimasto/a senza benzina *Sono reaymahsto/ah saynzah bayndzeenah*
I've locked the keys____ in the car	Ho chiuso le chiavi in macchina *O keeoozo lay keeahvee een mahkkeenah*
The car/motorbike/ ____ moped won't start	La macchina/la moto (cicletta) /il motorino non parte *Lah mahkkeenah/lah moto (cheeklayttah)/eel motoreeno non pahrtay*
Could you contact the _ breakdown service for me, please?	Può chiamarmi il soccorso stradale? *Pwo keeeahmahrmee eel sokkorso strahdahlay?*
Could you call a garage for me, please?	Può chiamarmi un garage? *Pwo keeeahmahrmee oon gahrahj?*
Could you give me____ a lift to...?	Mi darebbe un passaggio fino... ? *Mee dahraybbay oon pahssahdjo feeno...?*
– to the nearest garage?	– al prossimo garage? *– ahl prosseemo gahraj?*
– to the nearest town? _	– fino alla prossima città? *– feeno ahllah prosseemah cheettah?*
– to the nearest _____ telephone booth?	– fino al prossimo telefono pubblico? *– feeno ahl prosseemo taylayfono poobbleeko?*
– to the nearest _____ emergency phone?	– fino al prossimo telefono di emergenza? *– feeno ahl posseemo taylayfono dee aymayrjayntzah?*
Can we take my _____ moped?	Può caricare il mio motorino? *Pwo kahreekahray eel meeo motoreeno?*
Could you tow me to____ a garage?	Può trainarmi a un garage? *Pwo traheenahrmee ah oon gahrahj?*

English	Italian
There's probably_____ something wrong with...(See 5.5 and 5.8)	Probabilmente si è guastato/a/si sono guastati/e... _Probahbeelmayntay see ay gwahstahto/ah see sono gwahstahtee/ay..._
Can you fix it? _____	Me lo potrebbe aggiustare? _May lo potraybbay ahdjoostahray?_
Could you fix my tyre? _	Mi potrebbe aggiustare la gomma? _Mee potraybbay ahdjoostahray lah gommah?_
Could you change this _ wheel?	Potrebbe cambiare questa ruota? _Potraybbay kahmbeeahray kwaystah rwotah?_
Can you fix it so it'll_____ get me to...?	Me lo potrebbe aggiustare in modo da poter arrivare fino a...? _May lo potraybbay ahdjoostahray een modo dah potayr ahrreevahray feeno ah...?_
Which garage can _____ help me?	Quale altro garage potrebbe aiutarmi? _Kwahlay ahltro gahrahj potraybbay aheeootahrmee?_
When will my car/ _____ bicycle be ready?	La mia macchina/bicicletta, quando sarà pronta? _Lah meeah mahkkeenah/beecheeklettah kwahndo sahrah prontah?_
Have you already _____ finished?	Ha già finito? _Hah djah feeneeto?_
Can I wait for it here? _	Posso restare qui ad aspettare? _Posso raystahray kwee ahdahspayttahray?_
How much will it cost? _	Quanto verrà a costare? _Kwahnto vayrrah ah costahray?_
Could you itemise _____ the bill?	Mi potrebbe dettagliare il conto? _Mee potraybbay dayttahllyahray eel konto?_
Could you give me a ___ receipt for insurance purposes?	Mi potrebbe dare una ricevuta per l'assicurazione? _Mee potraybbay dahray oonah reechayvootah payr lahsseekoorahtzeeonay?_

5.8 The bicycle/moped

● **Cycle paths** are rare in Italy. Bikes can be hired in most Italian towns. Not much consideration for bikes should be expected on the roads. The maximum speed for mopeds is 40km/h but you should be aged 14 and over. Wearing a crash helmet is compulsory for both driver and passenger.

Mi mancano i pezzi di ricambio per la Sua macchina/bicicletta	I don't have parts for your car/bicycle
Devo andare a prendere i pezzi di ricambio altrove	I have to get the parts from somewhere else
Devo ordinare i pezzi di ricambio	I have to order the parts
Ci vorrà una mezza giornata	That'll take half a day
Ci vorrà un giorno	That'll take a day
Ci vorrà qualche giorno	That'll take a few days
Ci vorrà una settimana	That'll take a week
La macchina ha dei danni irreparabili	Your car is a write-off
Non si può riparare	It can't be repaired
La macchina/la moto(cicletta)/il motorino/la bicicletta sarà pronta alle...	The car/motor bike/moped/bicycle will be ready at... o'clock

5.9 Renting a vehicle

I'd like to rent a... _____	**Vorrei noleggiare un/una...**
	Vorray nolaydgeeahray oon/oonah...
Do I need a (special) ____ licence for that?	**Mi occorre una patente speciale?**
	Mee okkorray oonah pahtayntay spaych-eeahlay?
I'd like to rent the...for...	**Vorrei noleggiare il/la... per...**
	Vorrayee nolaydgeeahray eel/lah...payr...
the...for a day _____	**il/la... per un giorno**
	eel/lah...payr oon jorno
the...for two days _____	**il/la... per due giorni**
	eel/lah...payr dooay jornee
How much is that per __ day/week?	**Quanto costa al giorno/alla settimana?**
	Kwahnto kostah ahl jorno/ahllah saytteemahnah?
How much is the _____ deposit?	**Quant'è la cauzione?**
	Kwahnto ay lah kahootzeeonay?
Could I have a receipt__ for the deposit?	**Mi potrebbe dare una ricevuta per la cauzione?**
	Mee potraybbay dahray oonah reechayhvootah payr lah kahootzeeonay?
How much is the _____ surcharge per kilometre?	**Quant'è il supplemento di prezzo al chilometro?**
	Kwahnto ay eel soopplaymaynto dee praytzo ahl keelomayhtro?
Does that include _____ petrol?	**E' compresa la benzina?**
	Ay kompraysah lah bayndzeenah?
Does that include_____ insurance?	**E' compresa l'assicurazione?**
	Ay compraysah laysseekoorahtzeeonay?

What time can I pick ___ the...up?	A che ora potrei venire a prendere il/la...? *Ah kay orah potrayee vayneeray ah prayndayray eel/lah...?*
When does the...have ___ to be back?	A che ora dovrò riportare il/la...? *Ah kay orah dovro reeportahray eel/lah...?*
Where's the petrol tank?	Dov'è il serbatoio? *Dovay eel sayrbahtoeeo?*
What sort of fuel does___ it take?	Quale carburante occorre? *Kwahlay kahrboorahntay okkorray?*

5.10 Hitchhiking

Where are you _____ heading?	Dove va? *Dovay vah?*
Can you give me a lift? _	Mi dà un passaggio? *Mee dah oon pahssahdjo?*
Can my friend (m/f) ____ come too?	Darebbe un passaggio anche al mio amico/alla mia amica? *Dahraybbay oon pahssahdjo ahnkay ahl meeo ahmeeko/ahllah meeah ahmeekah?*
I'd like to go to... _____	Voglio andare a... *Vollyo ahndahray ah...*
Is that on the way _____ to...?	Si trova sulla strada per...? *See trovah soollah strahda payr...?*
Could you drop me ____ off...?	Mi potrebbe far scendere...? *Mee potraybbay fahr shayndayray...?*
Could you drop me off _ here?	Mi potrebbe far scendere qui? *Mee potraybbay fahr shayndayray kwee?*
– at the entrance to ___ the motorway?	– all'entrata dell'autostrada? *– ahll'ayntrahtah dayllowtostrahdah?*
– in the centre?_____	– al centro? *– ahl chayntro?*
– at the next _____ intersection?	– al prossimo incrocio? *– ahl prosseemo eenkrocheeo?*

Could you stop here, please?	Si potrebbe fermare qui per favore?
	See potraybbay fayrmahray kwee payr fahvoray?
I'd like to get out here	Vorrei scendere qui
	Vorrayee shayndayray kwee
Thanks for the lift	Grazie per il passaggio
	Grahtzeeay payr eel pahssahdjo

6

Public transport

6.1 In general

● **Bus tickets** are purchased at tobacconists, newspaper stands and automatic vending machines at major bus stops, then validated in a machine as you enter the bus. Single tickets be bought in blocks of four. Milan and Rome also have an underground train (*metropolitana*). Venice is served by a water-bus (*vaporetto*). Tickets are purchased from booths at most landing stations and validated before you get on the boat. A 24-hour ticket is good value for unlimited travel. Venice also has a gondola service (*traghetto*) crossing the Grand Canal, costing very little.

Il treno per... delle ore... viaggia con un ritardo di (circa)...minuti	The [time] train to...has been delayed by (about)...minutes
E' in arrivo sul binario...il treno per...	The train to...is now arriving at platform...
E' in arrivo sul binario...il treno proveniente da...	The train from...is now arriving at platform...
E' in partenza dal binario...il treno per...	The train to...will leave from platform...
Oggi il treno per... delle ore...partirà dal binario...	Today the [time] train to...will leave from platform...
La prossima stazione è...	The next station is...

Where does this train ___ go to?	Dove va questo treno?
	Dovay vah kwaysto trayno?
Does this boat go ___ to...?	Questo traghetto va a...?
	Kwaysto trahgaytto vah ah...?
Can I take this bus ___ to...?	Posso prendere questo autobus per andare a...?
	Posso prayndayray kwaysto ahootoboos payr ahndahray ah...?

Does this train stop at...?	Questo treno si ferma a...?
	Kwaysto trayno see fayrmah ah...?
Is this seat taken/free /reserved?	E' occupato/libero/prenotato questo posto?
	Ay okkoopahto/leebayro/praynotahto kwaysto posto?
I've booked...	Ho prenotato...
	O praynotahto...
Could you tell me where I have to get off for... ?	Mi potrebbe indicare la fermata per...?
	Mee potraybbay eendeekahray lah fayrmahtah payr...?
Could you let me know when we get to...?	Mi potrebbe avvisare quando arriviamo a...?
	Mee potraybbay ahvveezahray kwahndo ahrreeveeahmo ah...?
Could you stop at the next stop, please?	Si potrebbe fermare alla prossima fermata?
	See potraybbay fayrmahray ahllah prosseemah fayrmahtah?
Where are we?	Dove siamo?
	Dovay seeahmo?
Do I have to get off here?	Devo scendere adesso?
	Dayvo shayndayray ahdaysso?
Have we already passed...?	Abbiamo già passato...?
	Ahbbeeahmo jah pahssahto ..?
How long have I been asleep?	Quanto tempo ho dormito?
	Kwahnto taympo o dormeeto?
How long does the train stop here?	Quanto tempo si fermerà il treno?
	Kwahnto taympo see fayrmayrah eel trayno?
Can I come back on the same ticket?	Questo biglietto è valido anche per il viaggio di ritorno?
	Kwaysto beellyaytto ay vahleedo ahnkay payr eell veeahdjo dee reetorno?
Can I change on this ticket?	Posso cambiare con questo biglietto?
	Posso kahmbeeahray con kwaysto beellyaytto?

How long is this ticket__ valid for?	Quanto tempo è valido questo biglietto?
	Kwahnto taympo ay vahleedo kwaysto beellyaytto?
How much is the _____ supplement for the high speed train?	Quant'è il supplemento rapido?
	Kwahntò ay eel soopplaymaynto rahpeedo?

6.2 Questions to passengers

Ticket types

Prima o seconda classe?	First or second class?
Andata o andata e ritorno?	Single or return?
Fumatori o non fumatori?	Smoking or non-smoking?
Vicino al finestrino?	Window seat?
In testa o in coda?	Front or back (of train)?
Un posto o una cuccetta?	Seat or couchette?
Sopra, in mezzo o sotto?	Top, middle or bottom?
Classe turistica o prima classe?	Economy or first class?
Una cabina o un posto a sedere?	Cabin or seat?
Una cabina singola o per due?	Single or double?
Quanti siete a viaggiare?	How many are travelling?

Destination

Dove va?	Where are you travelling?
Quando parte?	When are you leaving?
La partenza è alle...	Your...leaves at...
Deve cambiare	You have to change
Deve scendere a...	You have to get off at...
Deve passare per...	You have to go via....
L'andata è il...	The outward journey is on...
Il ritorno è il...	The return journey is on...
Deve imbarcarsi entro...	You have to be on board by....(o'clock)

Inside the vehicle

Biglietti prego	Tickets, please
La prenotazione prego	Your reservation, please
Passaporto prego	Your passport, please
Ha sbagliato posto	You're in the wrong seat
Ha sbagliato...	You have made a mistake/You are in the wrong...
Questo posto è prenotato	This seat is reserved
Deve pagare un supplemento	You'll have to pay a supplement
Il/la... viaggia con un ritardo di... minuti	The...has been delayed by...minutes

6.3 Tickets

Where can I...?	Dove posso...?
	Dovay posso...?
– buy a ticket?	Dove posso comprare un biglietto?
	– komprahray oon beellyaytto?
– reserve a seat?	Dove posso prenotare un posto?
	– praynotahray oon posto?
– book a flight?	Dove posso prenotare un volo?
	– praynotahray oon volo?
Could I have...for... please?	Mi può dare...per...per favore
	Mee pwo dahray...payr...payr fahvoray
A single to...please	Un'andata per...per favore
	Oonahndahtah payr...payr fahvoray
A return ticket, please	Un'andata e ritorno, per favore
	Oonahndahtah ay reetorno payr fahvoray
first class	prima classe
	preemah klahssay
second class	seconda classe
	saykondah klahssay
economy class	classe turistica
	klahssay tooreesteekah
I'd like to book a seat/couchette/cabin	Vorrei prenotare un posto/una cuccetta/una cabina
	Vorrayee praynotahray oon posto/oonah cootchayttah/oonah kahbeenah
I'd like to book a top/middle/bottom berth in the sleeping car	Vorrei prenotare un posto nella carrozza letto in alto/in mezzo/in basso
	Vorrayee praynotahray oon posto nayllah kahrrotzah laytto een ahlto/een maydzo/een bahsso
smoking/no smoking	fumatori/non fumatori
	foomahtoree/non foomahtoree
by the window	vicino al finestrino
	veecheeno ahl feenaystreeno

single/double _____	singola/per due
	seengolah/payr dooay
at the front/back_____	nella parte davanti/in fondo
	nayllah pahrtay dahvahntee/een fondo
There are...of us _____	Siamo in...
	Seeahmo een...
We have a car_____	Abbiamo una macchina
	Ahbbeeahmo oonae makkeenah
We have a caravan ____	Abbiamo una roulotte
	Ahbbeeahmo oonah roolot
We have...bicycles _____	Abbiamo...biciclette
	Ahbbeeahmo...beecheeklayttay
Do you have a... _____	Ha un/una ?
	Ah oon/oonah...?
– travel card for _____	Ha una tessera valida dieci corse?
10 trips?	*Ah oonah tayssayrah vahleedah deeaychee*
	corsay?
– weekly travel card?___	Ha un abbonamento settimanale
	Ah oon ahbbonahmaynto
	saytteemahnahlay?
– monthly season	Ha un abbonamento mensile?
ticket? _____	*Ah oon ahbbonahmaynto maynseelay?*
Where's-? _____	Dov'è ?
	Dovay ay?
Where's the information	Dov'è l'ufficio informazioni?
desk?	*Dovay ay looffeecheeo*
	eenformahtzeeonee?

6.4 Information

Where can I find a _____	Dov'è l'orario delle partenze/degli arrivi?
timetable?	*Dovay ay lorayryo dayllay*
	pahrtayntzay/daylly ahrreevee?
Where's the...desk? ____	Dov'è il banco di...
	Dovay eel bahnko dee...

Do you have a city map with the bus/the underground routes on it?	Avrebbe una pianta della città con le linee degli autobus/del metrò?
	Ahvraybbay oonah peeahntah dayllah cheettah kon lay leenayay daylly ahootoboos/dayl maytro?
Do you have a timetable?	Avrebbe un orario?
	Ahvraybbay oon orayreeo?
Will I get my money back?	Le spese mi saranno rimborsate?
	Lay spaysay mee sahrahnno reemborsahtay?
I'd like to confirm/ cancel/change my booking for/trip to...	Vorrei confermare/annullare/cambiare la prenotazione per...
	Vorrayee confayrmahray/ahnnoollahray/ kahmbyahray lah praynotahtzeeonay payr...
I'd like to go to... What is the quickest way to get there?	Vorrei andare a...Qual'è il modo più rapido per andarci?
	Vorrayee ahndahray ah...Kwahlay ay eel modo peeoo rahpeedo payr ahndahrchee?
How much is a single/return to...?	Quanto costa un'andata/un'andata e ritorno per...?
	Kwahnto kostah oonahndahtah/ oonahndahtah ay reetorno payr...?
Do I have to pay a supplement?	Devo pagare un supplemento?
	Dayvo pahgahray oon soopplaymaynto?
Can I break my journey with this ticket?	Posso interrompere il viaggio con questo biglietto?
	Posso eentayrrompayray eel veeahdjo con kwaysto beellyaytto?
How much luggage am I allowed?	Quanti chili di bagaglio posso portare ?
	Kwahntee keely dee bahgahllyo posso portahray?
Is this a direct train?	E' un treno diretto?
	Ay oon trayno deeraytto?
Do I have to change? Where?	Devo cambiare? Dove?
	Dayvo kahmbeeahray? Dovay?

Does the plane touch __ down anywhere?	L'aereo fa scalo da nessuna parte? *Lahayrayo fah skahlo dah nayssoonah pahrtay?*
Will there be any _____ stopovers?	Ci saranno soste intermedie? *Chee sahrahnno sostay eentayrmaydeeay?*
Does the boat stop ____ at any other ports on the way?	Il traghetto fa scalo ad altri porti? *Eel trahgaytto fah skahlo ahdahltree portee?*
Does the train/ _____ bus stop at...?	Questo treno/autobus si ferma a...? *Kwaysto trayno/ahootoboos see fayrmah ah...?*
Where do I get off? ____	Dove devo scendere? *Dovay dayvo shayndayray?*
Is there a connection____ to...?	C'è una coincidenza per...? *Chay oonah coeencheedayntzah payr...?*
How long do I have to__ wait?	Quanto tempo devo aspettare? *Kwahnto taympo dayvo ahspayttahray?*
When does...leave? ____	Quando parte...? *Kwahndo pahrtay...?*
What time does the ____ first/next/last...leave?	A che ora parte il/la primo/a/il/la prossimo/a/l'ultimo/a...? *Ah kay orah pahrtay eel/lah preemo/ah eel/lah prosseemo/ah/loolteemo/ah...?*
How long does...take? _	Quanto tempo impiega...? *Kwahnto taympo eempeeaygah...?*
What time does...arrive_ in...?	A che ora arriverà...a...? *Ah kay orah ahrreevayhrah...ah...?*
Where does the...to... __ leave from?	Da dove parte il/la...per...? *Dah dovay pahrtay eel/lah...payr...?*
Is this the train/_____ bus...to...?	E' questo il treno/l'autobus per...? *Ay kwaysto eel trayno/lahootoboos payr...?*

6.5 Aeroplanes

● **On arrival** at an Italian airport (*aeroporto*), you will find the following signs:

accettazione	internazionale	voli domestici
check-in	international	domestic flights
arrivo	partenze	
arrivals	departenze	
	departures	

6.6 Trains

● **Train travel** in Italy is simple and cheap. *The Ferrovie dello Stato* (FS) is the state rail system. There are several types of trains: the *regionale* stops at all stations and is slow; the *interregionale* travels between regions; the *diretto* means you reach your destination without having to change; the *espresso* stops at major stations. The ETR450, or *Pendolino*, is an espress service between Rome, Florence, Bologna and Milan; the *Intercity* services major cities and the *EuroCity* connects major European cities. Tickets must be punched by a validation machine at the entrance to platforms.

6.7 Taxis

● **There are plenty of taxis** in Italian cities but they are quite expensive. They can be found on ranks, especially at train and bus stations, or you can phone the radio-taxi numbers from a rank or any telephone. Rates vary and there is a supplement from 10pm to 7am and on Sundays and bank holidays. Check for airport supplements.

libero	occupato	posteggio dei taxi
for hire	occupied	taxi rank

Taxi! _____	Taxi!
	Tahxee!
Could you get me a ___ taxi, please?	Mi potrebbe chiamare un taxi?
	Mee potraybbay keeahmahray oon tahxee?
Where can I find a taxi _ around here?	Dove posso prendere un taxi qui vicino?
	Dovay posso prayndaray oon tahxee kwee veecheeno?
Could you take me ____ to..., please?	Mi porti a... per favore
	Mee portee ah...payr fahvoray
Could you take me to _ this address, please	Mi porti a questo indirizzo per favore
	Mee portee ah kwaysto eendeereetzo payr fahvoray
– to the...hotel, please _	Mi porti all'albergo...per favore
	Mee portee ahllahlbayrgo...payr fahvoray
– to the town/city ____ centre, please	Mi porti al centro per favore
	Mee portee ahl chayntro payr fahvoray
– to the station, please _	Mi porti alla stazione per favore
	Mee portee ahllah statzeeonay payr fahvoray
– to the airport, please _	Mi porti all'aeroporto per favore
	Mee portee ahllahayroporto payr fahvoray
How much is the _____ trip to...?	Quanto costa una corsa fino a...?
	Kwahnto kostah oonah korsah feeno ah...?
How far is it to...?_____	Quanto è lontano...?
	Kwahnto ay lontahno...?
Could you turn on the _ meter, please?	Può accendere il tassametro, per piacere?
	Pwo ahtchayndayray eel tahssahmaytro, payr peeahchayray?
I'm in a hurry_____	Ho fretta
	O frayttah
Could you speed up/___ slow down a little?	Può andare più veloce/piano?
	Pwo ahndahray peeoo vayhlochay/peeahno?
Could you take a _____ different route?	Può prendere un'altra strada?
	Pwo prayndayray oonahltrah strahdah?

I'd like to get out here, _ please.	Mi faccia scendere adesso *Mee fahtchhah shayndayray ahdaysso*
Go - _____	Vada *Vahdah*
You have to go...here __	Deve andare... qui *Dayvay ahndahray... kwee*
Go straight ahead _____	Vada dritto *Vahdah dreetto*
Turn left _____	Vada a sinistra *Vahda ah seeneestra*
Turn right _____	Vada a destra *Vahdah ah daystrah*
This is it/We're here ____	Siamo arrivati *Seeahmo ahrreevahtee*
Could you wait a _____ minute for me, please?	Mi potrebbe aspettare un attimo? *Mee potraybbay ahspayttahray oon ahtteemo?*

7.1 General

● **There is a great variety** of accommodation in Italy. A hotel or *albergo* can be awarded up to five stars while a *pensione* will usually be one to three star quality. *Locande* are similar to *pensioni*, and *alloggi* or *affittacamere* are usually cheaper and are not part of the star classification system. Some youth hostels, *ostelli per la gioventù*, offer family rooms. *Agriturismo* is the popular practice of staying in farmhouses or at a restaurant with rooms. A network of *rifugi* offers dormitory accommodation in the Alps, Appenines or other mountains in Italy. Campsites range from large complexes to simple grounds. Free camping is not permitted in Italy, you need the permission of the landowner to camp on private property.

My name is...I've made a reservation	Il mio nome è...Ho prenotato *Eel meeo nomay ay...O praynotahto*
How much is it per night/week/ month?	Quanto costa per una notte/alla settimana/al mese? *Kwahnto kostah payr oonah nottay/ahllah saytteemahnah/ahl maysay?*
We'll be staying at least...nights/weeks	Vogliamo rimanere minimo...notti/settimane *Vollyahmo reemahnayray meeneemo...nottee/setteemahnay*
We don't know yet	Non lo sappiamo di preciso *Non lo sahppeeahmo dee praycheezo*

Quanto tempo vuole rimanere?	How long will you be staying?
Mi compili questo modulo, per favore	Fill out this form, please
Potrei avere il Suo passaporto?	Could I see your passport?
Deve pagare una caparra	I'll need a deposit
Deve pagare in anticipo	You'll have to pay in advance

Do you allow pets _____ (cats/dogs)?	Sono permessi gli animali domestici (cani/gatti)?
	Sono payrmayssee lly ahneemahlee domaysteechee (kahnee/gahttee)?
What time does the _____ gate/door open/close?	A che ora apre/chiude il cancello?
	Ah kay orah ahpray/keeoooday eel kahnchello?
Could you get me _____ a taxi, please?	Mi potrebbe chiamare un taxi?
	Mee potraybbay keeahmahray oon tahxee?
Is there any mail _____ for me?	C'è posta per me?
	Chay postah payr may?

7.2 Camping

Scelga pure un posto	You can pick your own site
Le verrà indicato un posto	You'll be allocated a site
Ecco il numero del Suo posto	This is your site number
Attacchi bene questo sulla macchina per favore	Please stick this firmly to your car
Non perda questa tesserina	You mustn't lose this card

Where's the manager? _	Dov'è l'amministratore?
	Dovay ay lahmmeenneestrahtoray?
Are we allowed to _____ camp here?	E' permesso fare il campeggio qui?
	Ay payrmaysso fahray eel kahmpaydjo kwee?
There are...of us and _____ we have...tents	Siamo in...e abbiamo...tende
	Seeahmo een...ay ahbbeeahmo...taynday
Can we pick our _____ own site?	Possiamo scegliere noi un posto?
	Posseeahmo shayllyayhray noee oon posto?
Do you have a quiet _____ spot for us?	Ha un posto tranquillo per noi?
	Ah oon posto trahnkweello payr noy?

Do you have any other sites available?	Non c'è un altro posto libero?
	Non chay oonahltro posto leebayro?
It's too windy/sunny/shady here.	C'è troppo vento/troppo sole/troppa ombra qui
	Chay troppo vaynto/troppo solay/troppah ombrah kwee
It's too crowded here	C'è troppa gente qui
	Chay troppah jayntay kwee
The ground's too hard/uneven	La terra è troppo dura/ineguale
	Lah tayhrrah ay troppo doorah/eenaygwahlay
Do you have a level spot for the camper/caravan/folding caravan?	Ha un posto piano per il nostro camper/la nostra roulotte/il nostro carrello tenda?
	Ah oon posto peeahno payr eel nostro kahmper/lah nostrah roolot/eel nostro kahrrayllo tayndah?
Could we have adjoining sites?	E' possibile avere posti vicini?
	Ay posseebeelay ahvayray postee veecheenee?
Can we park the car next to the tent?	E' permesso parcheggiare la macchina vicino alla tenda?
	Ay payrmaysso pahrkaydjahray lah mahkkeenah veecheeno ahllah tayndah?
How much is it per person/tent/caravan/car?	Quanto costa per persona/per una tenda/per una roulotte/per una macchina?
	Kwahnto kostah payr payrsonah/payr oonah tayndah/payr oonah roolot/payr oonah mahkkeenah?
Do you have chalets for hire?	Ha uno chalet da affittare?
	Ah oono shahlay dah ahffeettahray?
Are there any...?	Ci sono...?
	Chee sono...?
– hot showers?	Ci sono docce calde?
	Chee sono dotchay kahlday?
– washing machines?	Ci sono lavatrici?
	Chee sono lahvahtreechee?

Camping equipment

luggage space	lo spazio per bagaglio	*lo spahzeeo payr bahgahllyo*
can opener	apriscatole (m)	*ahpreeskahtolay*
butane gas bottle	bombola a gas butano	*bombolah ah gahs bootahno*
pannier	sacca	*sahkkah*
gas cooker	fornello da campeggio	*fornayllo dah kahmpaydjeeo*
groundsheet	fondo della tenda	*fondo dayllah tayndah*
mallet	martello di gomma	*mahrtayllo dee gommah*
hammock	amaca	*ahmahkah*
jerry can	tanica	*tahneekah*
campfire	fuoco	*fwoko*
folding chair	seggiolino pieghevole	*saydjoleeno peeaygayvolay*
insulated picnic box	borsa frigo	*borsah freego*
ice pack	accumulatore (m) di ghiaccio	*ahkkoomoolahtoray dee geeahtcheeo*
compass	bussola	*boossolah*
corkscrew	cavatappi	*kahvahtahppee*
airbed	materassino gonfiabile	*mahtayrahsseeno gonfeeahbeelay*

Is there a...on the site?	Il campeggio ha...? *Eel kahmpaydjo ah...?*
Is there a children's play area on the site?	Il campeggio ha un parco giochi? *Eel kamppaydjo ah oon pahrko jokee?*
Are there covered cooking facilities on the site?	C'è un' area coperta per cucinare? *Chay oonahrayah kopayrtah payr koocheenahray?*
Can I rent a safe?	E' possibile prendere a noleggio una cassetta di sicurezza? *Ay posseebeelay prayndayray ah nolaydjo oonah kahssayttah dee seekooraytzah?*

airbed pump	pompa	*pompah*
awning	tenda	*tayndah*
sleeping bag	sacco a pelo	*sahkko ah paylo*
saucepan	pentola	*payntohlah*
handle (pan)	manico	*mahneeko*
primus stove	fornello a spirito	*fornayllo ah speereeto*
zip	chiusura lampo	*keeoozoorah lahmpo*
backpack	zaino	*dzaheeno*
guy rope	tirante (m) di tenda	*teerahntay dee tayndah*
storm lantern	lanterna a vento	*lahntayrnah ah vaynto*
camp bed	brandina	*brahndeenah*
table	tavolino	*tahvoleeno*
tent	tenda	*tayndah*
tent peg	picchetto	*peekkaytto*
tent pole	palo	*pahloh*
thermos flask	il termos	*eel tayrmoss*
water bottle	borraccia	*borrahtchah*
clothes peg	molletta	*mollayttah*
clothes line	corda da bucato	*kordah dah bookahto*
windbreak	paravento	*pahrahvaynto*
torch	torcia	*torchah*
penknife	temperino	*taympayreeno*

Are we allowed to ___ barbecue here?	E' permesso fare il barbecue?	
	Ay payrmaysso fahray eel bahrbaykeeoo?	
Are there any power ___ points?	Ci sono delle prese elettriche?	
	Chee sono dayllay praysay aylayttreekay?	
Is there drinking ___ water?	C'è acqua potabile?	
	Chay ahkwah potahbeelay?	
When's the rubbish ___ collected?	Quando c'è la raccolta dei rifiuti?	
	Kwahndo chay lah rahkkoltah dayèe reefeeootee?	

Do you sell gas bottles _ Vende delle bombole di gas (gas
(butane gas/ butano/gas propano)? '
propane gas)? *Vaynday dayllay bombolay dee gahs (gahs bootahno/gahs propahno)?*

7.3 Hotel/B&B/apartment/holiday house

Do you have a single/ __ Ha una camera singola/doppia?
double room *Ah oonah kahmayhrah*
available? *seengolah/doppeeah?*

Il bagno e la doccia sono allo	The toilet and shower are on the
stesso piano/nella Sua camera	same floor/en suite
Prego, da questa parte	This way please
La Sua camera è al...piano,	Your room is on the...floor,
numero...	number...

---

per person/per room ___ per persona/per camera
payr payrsonah/payr kahmayhrah

Does that include_____ E' inclusa la prima colazione?/E' incluso il
breakfast/lunch/ pranzo?/E' inclusa la cena?
dinner? *Ay eenkloosah lah preemah kolahtzeeonay?/ Ay eenklooso eel prahntzo?/Ay eenkloosah lah chaynah?*

Could we have two ____ E' possibile stare in due camere vicine?
adjoining rooms? *Ay posseebeelay stahray een dooay kahmayray veecheenay?*

with/without_____ con/senza gabinetto/bagno/doccia
toilet/bath/shower *con/saynzah gahbeenaytto/bahneeo/dotchah*

facing the street _____ guarda sulla strada
gwahrdah soollah strahdah

at the back _____	sul retro
	sool raytro
with/without sea view _	che dà/che non dà sul mare
	kay dah/kay non dah sool mahray
Is there...in the hotel? _	L'albergo ha...?
	Lahlbayrgo hah...?
Is there a lift in the _____ hotel?	L'albergo ha l'ascensore?
	Lahlbayrgo ah lahshaynsoray?
Do you have room _____ service?	C'è il servizio in camera?
	Chay eel sayrveetzeeo een kahmayhrah?
Could I see the room? _	E' possibile vedere la camera?
	Ay posseebeelay vahdayray lah kahmayrah?
I'll take this room _____	Prendo questa
	Prayndo kwaystah
We don't like this one _	Questa qui non ci piace
	Kwaystah kwee non chee peeahchay
Do you have a larger/ _ less expensive room?	Ha una camera più grande/meno cara?
	Ah oonah kahmayhrah peeoo grahnday/mayno kahrah?
Could you put in a _____ cot?	Potrebbe aggiungere un lettino per il bambino/la bambina?
	Potraybbay ahdjoonjayray oon laytteeno payr eel bahmbeeno/lah bahmbeenah?
What time's breakfast? _	A che ora c'è la colazione?
	Ah kay orah chay lah kolahtzeeonay?
Where's the dining _____ room?	Dov'è la sala da pranzo?
	Dovay ay la sahlah dah prahntzo?
Can I have breakfast ___ in my room?	Mi potrebbe portare la prima colazione in camera?
	Mee potraybbay portahray lah preemah kolahtzeeonay een kahmayhrah?
Where's the _____ emergency exit/fire escape?	Dov'è l'uscita di sicurezza/la scala di sicurezza?
	Dovay ay loosheetah dee seekooraytzah/lah skahlah dee seekooretzah?

101

Where can I park my ___ car (safely)?	Dove posso parcheggiare la mia macchina (in un posto sicuro)?
	Dovay posso pahrkaydjahray lah meeah mahkkeenah (een oon posto seekooro)?
The key to room...,_____ please	La chiave della camera...per favore
	Lah keeahvay dayllah kahmayhrah...payr fahvoray
Could you put this in ___ the safe, please?	Posso mettere questo nella sua cassetta di sicurezza?
	Posso mayttayray kwaysto naylla sooah kahssayttah dee seekooraytzah?
Could you wake me_____ at...tomorrow?	Mi potrebbe svegliare domani alle...?
	Mee potraybbay svayllyahray domahnee ahllay...?
Could you find a_____ babysitter for me?	Mi potrebbe cercare una babysitter?
	Mee potraybbay chayrkahray oonah bahbeeseettayr?
Could I have an extra ___ blanket?	Potrei avere un'altra coperta?
	Potray ahvayhray oonahltrah copayrtah?
What days do the_____ cleaners come in?	Che giorno fanno le pulizie?
	Kay jorno fahnno lay pooleetzeeay?
When are the sheets/ ___ towels/tea towels changed?	Quando cambiano le lenzuola/gli asciugamani/gli strofinacci?
	Kwahndo kahmbeeahno lay layntzwolah/lly ahshoogahmahnee/lly strofeenahtchee?

7.4 Complaints

We can't sleep for _____ the noise	Non riusciamo a dormire per i rumori
	Non reeoosheeahmo ah dormeeray payr ee roomoree
Could you turn the_____ radio down, please?	Può abbassare la radio?
	Pwo ahbbahssahray lah rahdeeo?
We're out of toilet paper	E' finita la carta igienica
	Ay feeneetah lah kahrtah eejayneekah

There aren't any.../ _____ there's not enough...	Non ci sono/ci sono troppo pochi/e... *Non chee sono/chee sono troppo pokee/ay...*
The bed linen's dirty _____	La biancheria è sporca *Lah beeahnkayreeyah ay sporkah*
The room hasn't been _____ cleaned.	La camera non è stata pulita *La kahmayrah non ay stahtah pooleetah*
The kitchen is not _____ clean	La cucina non è pulita *Lah koocheenah non ay pooleetah*
The kitchen utensils are dirty	Gli utensili da cucina sono sporchi *Lly ootaynseelee dah koocheenah sono sporkee*
The heating isn't _____ working	Il riscaldamento non funziona *Eel reeskahldahmaynto non foontzeeoonah*
There's no (hot)_____ water/electricity	Non c'è acqua (calda)/corrente *Non chay ahkwah (kahldah)/corrayntay*
...doesn't work/is _____ broken	...non funziona/è rotto/a *...non foontzeeoonah/ay rotto/ah*
Could you have that _____ seen to?	Potrebbe farlo aggiustare? *Potraybbay fahrlo ahdjoostahray?*
Could I have another_____ room/site?	Posso cambiare camera/posto per la tenda? *Posso kahmbeeahray kahmayra/posto payr lah tayndah?*
The bed creaks terribly _	Il letto scricchiola terribilmente *Eel laytto skreekkeeolah tayrreebeelmayntay*
The bed sags _____	Il letto cede troppo *Eel laytto chayday troppo*
Could I have a board_____ under the mattress?	Mi potrebbe dare una tavola da mettere sotto il materasso? *Mee potraybbay dahray oonah tahvolah dah mayttayray sotto eel mahtayrahsso?*
It's too noisy _____	C'è troppo rumore *Chay troppo roomoray*
There are a lot of _____ insects/bugs	Ci sono molti insetti *Chee sono moltee eensayttee*

This place is full of mosquitos	E' pieno di zanzare
	Ay peeayno dee zahnzahray
– cockroaches	E' pieno di scarafaggi
	Ay peeayno dee skahrahfahdjee

7.5 Departure

See also 8.2 Settling the bill

I'm leaving tomorrow. Could I settle my bill, please?	Domani parto. Mi potrebbe fare il conto adesso?
	Domahny pahrto. Mee potraybbay fahray eel konto ahdaysso?
What time should we vacate the room?	A che ora dobbiamo lasciare la camera?
	Ah kay orah dobbeeahmo lahsheeahray lah kahmayhrah?
Could I have my deposit/passport back, please?	Mi potrebbe riconsegnare la caparra/il passaporto?
	Mee potraybbay reekonsayneeahray lah kahpahrrah/eel pahssahporto?
We're in a great hurry	Abbiamo molta fretta
	Abbeeahrmo moltah frayttah
Could you forward my mail to this address?	Può rispedirmi la posta a questo indirizzo?
	Pwo reespaydeermee lah postah ah kwaysto eendeereeetzo?
Could we leave our luggage here until we leave?	Possiamo lasciare le nostre valigie qui finchè partiamo?
	Posseeahmo lahsheeahray lay nostray vahleedjay kwee feenkay pahrteeahmo?
Thanks for your hospitality	Grazie per l'ospitalità
	Grahtzeeay payr lospeetahleetah

8 Money matters

● **Banks:** are open Monday–Friday 8.30–1.30 and 2.30 –4.30. Proof of identity is usually required to exchange currency.

8.1 Banks

Where can I find a ____ bank/an exchange office around here?	Scusi, c'è una banca/un'agenzia di cambio qui vicino?
	Skoozee, chay oonah bahnkah/ oonahjayntzeeah dee kahmbeeo kwee veecheeno?
Where can I cash this ___ traveller's cheque/giro cheque?	Dove posso incassare questo traveller cheque/assegno postale?
	Dovay posso eenkahssahray kwaysto trahvayllayr shayk/ahssayneeo postahlay?
Can I cash this...here? _	E' possibile incassare qui questo/a...
	Ay posseebeelay eenkahssahray kwee kwaysto/ah...?
Can I withdraw money _ on my credit card here?	E' possibile prelevare qui dei soldi con una carta di credito?
	Ay posseebeelay praylayvahray kwee dayee soldee con oonah kahrtah dee craydeeto?

Firmi qui per favore	Sign here, please
Compili questo modulo per favore	Fill this out, please
Potrei vedere il Suo passaporto?	Could I see your passport, please?
Potrei vedere la Sua carta d'identità?	Could I see your identity card, please?
Potrei vedere la Sua carta assegni?	Could I see your cheque card, please?
Potrei vedere la Sua carta assegni?	Could I see your bank card, please?

What's the minimum/ __ maximum amount?	Qual'è la somma minima/massima?
	Kwahlay ay lah sommah meeneemah/mahsseemah?
Can I take out less_____ than that?	E' possibile prelevare una somma minore?
	Ay posseebeelay praylayvahray oonah sommah meenoray?
I had some money_____ cabled here. Has it arrived yet?	Ho fatto fare una rimessa per cablogramma. E' già arrivata?
	Oh fahtto fahray oona reemayssah payr kahblograhmmah. Ay jah ahrreevahtah?
These are the details ___ of my bank in the UK	Ecco i dati della mia banca in Inghilterra
	Ekko ee dahtee dayllah meeah bahnkah een Eengeeltayhrrah
This is the number of __ my bank/giro account	Ecco il numero del mio conto in banca/conto corrente postale
	Ekko eel noomayro dayl meeo konto een bahnkah/konto korrayntay postahlay
I'd like to change _____ some money	Vorrei cambiare dei soldi
	Vorrayee kahmbeeahray dayee soldee
– pounds into..._____	– sterline in... – *stayrleenay een...*
– dollars into... _____	– dollari in... – *dollahree een...*
What's the exchange___ rate?	Quant'è il cambio?
	Kwahnto ay eel kahmbeeo?
Could you give me_____ some small change with it?	Mi potrebbe dare anche degli spiccioli per favore?
	Mee potraybbay dahray ahnkay daylly speetchoholee payr fahvoray?
This is not right_____	C'è un errore
	Chay oonayrroray

8.2 Settling the bill

Could you put it on ____ my bill?	Lo metta sul mio conto
	Lo mayttah sool meeo konto

Is service included?	Il servizio è compreso?
	Eel sayrveetzeeo ay komprayso?
Can I pay by...?	Potrei pagare con...?
	Potrayee pahgahray kon...?
Can I pay by credit card?	Potrei pagare con una carta di credito?
	Potrayee pahgahray kon oonah kahrtah dee kraydeeto?
Can I pay by traveller's cheque?	Potrei pagare con un traveller cheque?
	Potrayee pahgahray kon oon trahvayller shayk?
Can I pay with foreign currency?	Potrei pagare con soldi stranieri?
	Potrayee pahgahray kon soldee straneeayree?
You've given me too much/you haven't given me enough change.	Mi ha dato troppo di resto/Non mi ha dato abbastanza di resto
	Mee ah dahto troppo dee raysto/Non mee ah dahto ahbbahstahnzah dee raysto
Could you check this again, please?	Potrebbe verificare di nuovo?
	Potraybbay vayhreefeekahray dee nwovo?
Could I have a receipt, please?	Mi potrebbe dare una ricevuta per favore?
	Mee potraybbay dahray oonah reechayvootah payr fahvoray?
I don't have enough money on me.	Non mi bastano i soldi
	Non mee bahstahno ee soldee
This is for you	Ecco a Lei
	Aykkoh ah lay
Keep the change	Tenga il resto
	Tayngah eel raysto

Non accettiamo carte di credito/traveller cheque/valuta straniera	We don't accept credit cards/traveller's cheques/foreign currency

9

Post and telephone

9.1 Post

For giros, see 8 Money matters

● **Major post offices** are open Monday to Saturday from 8.30am to 6 or 7pm. Smaller post offices open Monday to Friday, 8.30am to 2pm and on Saturdays from 8.30am to midday. Stamps (*francobolli*) can also be purchased at authorised tobacconists (*tabacchi*). The cost of sending a letter depends on its weight and the cost of sending an air mail letter also depends on where it is being sent. The Italian postal service is notoriously inefficient.

francobolli	telegrammi	vaglia postali
stamps	telegrammes	money orders
pacchi		
parcels		

Where is...? _____	Dov'è...?
	Dovay ay...?
– the nearest post _____ office?	Dov'è l'ufficio postale più vicino?
	Dovay ay looffeetcheeo postahlay peeoo veecheeno?
– the main post office __	Dov'è la posta centrale?
	Dovay ay lah postah chayntrahlay?
– the nearest post _____ box?	Dov'è la buca delle lettere più vicina?
	Dovay ay lah bookah dayllay layttayray peeoo veecheenah?
Which counter should __ I go to...?	A quale sportello devo rivolgermi?
	Ah kwahlay sportayllo dayvo reevoljayrmee?
Which counter should __ I go to to send a fax?	Lo sportello per fare un fax, qual è?
	Lo sportayllo payr fahray oon fahx, kwahlay?

Which counter should I go to to change money?	Lo sportello per cambiare dei soldi, qual è?
	Lo sportayllo payr kahmbyahray dayee soldee, kwahlay?
Which counter should I go to to change giro cheques?	Lo sportello per i vaglia di conto corrente postale, qual è?
	Lo sportayllo payr ee vahllyah dee konto korrayntay postahlay, kwahlay?
Which counter should I go to to cable a money order?	Lo sportello per fare una rimessa cablografica, qual è?
	Lo sportayllo payr fahray oonah reemayssah kahblografeekah, kwahlay?
Which counter should I go to for poste restante?	Lo sportello per il fermo posta, qual è?
	Lo sportayllo payr eel fayrmo postah, kwahlay?
Is there any mail for me? My name's...	C'è posta per me? Il mio nome è...?
	Chay postah payr may? Eel meeo nomay ay...

Stamps

What's the postage for a...to...?	Quanti francobolli ci vogliono per un/uno...da spedire a/in...?
	Kwahntee frahnkobollee chee vollyono payr oon/oonah...dah spaydeeray ah/een...?
Are there enough stamps on it?	Bastano questi francobolli?
	Bahstahno kwaystee frahnkobollee?
I'd like [quantity] [value] stamps	Vorrei...francobolli da...
	Vorrayee...frahnkobollee dah...
I'd like to send this...	Vorrei spedire questo/a...
	Vorrayee spaydeeray kwaysto/ah...
- express	Vorrei spedire questo/a per espresso
	Vorrayee spaydeeray kwaysto/ah payr ayspraysso
- by air mail	Vorrei spedire questo/a per posta aerea
	Vorrayee spaydeeray kwaysto/ah payr postah ahayrayah

| – by registered mail ____ | Vorrei spedire questo/a per raccomandata |
| | *Vorrayee spaydeeray kwaysto/ah payr rahkkomahndahtah* |

Telegram/fax

I'd like to send a_____ telegram to...	Vorrei spedire un telegramma a...
	Vorrayee spaydeeray oon taylaygrahmmah ah...
How much is that_____ per word?	Quanto costa per parola?
	Kwahnto kostah payr pahrolah?
This is the text I want __ to send	Ecco il testo che vorrei spedire
	Ekko eel taysto kay vorray spaydeeray
Shall I fill out the form __ myself?	Desidera che compili io il modulo?
	Dayzeedayhrah kay kompeelee eeo eel modoolo?
Can I make _____ photocopies/send a fax here?	E' possibile fare una fotocopia qui/spedire un fax da qui?
	Ay posseebeelay fahray oonah fotokopeeah kwee/spaydeeray oon fahx dah kwee?
How much is it _____ per page?	Quanto costa per pagina?
	Kwahnto kostah payr pahjeenah?

9.2 Telephone

See also 1.8 Telephone alphabet

● **Direct international calls** can easily be made from public telephones using a phonecard available from tobacconists (*tabacchi*), newspaper stands and vending machines in Telecom offices. Dial 00 to get out of Italy, then the relevant country code (UK 44; USA 1), city code and number. To make a reverse charge call from a public telephone, dial 170 for international and 15 for European countries. All operators speak English. When phoning someone in Italy, you will be greeted with *Pronto*.

Is there a phone box ___ around here?	Senta, c'è una cabina telefonica qui vicino?
	Sayntah, chay oonah kahbeenah taylayfoneekah kwee veecheeno?
May I use your _____ phone, please?	Scusi, potrei servirmi del Suo telefono?
	Skoozee, potrayee sayrveermee dayl soo-o taylayfono?
Do you have a _____ (city/region) phone directory?	Ha un elenco telefonico della città di/della regione...?
	Ah oonaylaynko taylayfoneeko dayllah cheettah dee..../dayllah rayjonay...?
Where can I get a_____ phone card?	Dove posso comprare una scheda telefonica?
	Dovay posso komprahray oonah skaydah taylayfoneekah?
Could you give me...? __	Mi potrebbe dare...?
	Mee potraybbay dahray...?
– the number for_____ international directory enquiries?	Mi potrebbe dare il numero dell'ufficio informazioni per l'estero?
	Mee potraybbay dahray eel noomayro dayll ooffeecheeo eenformahtzeeoonee payr laystayro?
– the number of _____ room...?	Mi potrebbe dare il numero della camera...?
	Mee potraybbay dahray eel noomayro dayllah kahmayrah...?
– the international _____ access code?	Mi potrebbe dare il prefisso internazionale?
	Mee potraybbay dahray eel prayfeesso eentayrnahtzeeoonahlay?
– the...(country) _____ code?	Mi potrebbe dare il prefisso per il/la...?
	Mee potraybbay dahray eel prayfeesso payr eel/lah...?
– the trunk code for...? _	Mi potrebbe dare il prefisso di...?
	Mee potraybbay dahray eel prayfeesso dee...?

113

– the number of _____ [subscriber]...?	Mi potrebbe dare il numero dell' abbonato...?
	Mee potraybbay dahray eel noomayro dayll' ahbbonahto...?
Could you check if this _ number's correct?	Potrebbe verificare se questo numero è giusto?
	Potraybbay vayhreefeekahray say kwaysto noomayro ay joosto?
Can I dial international _ direct?	E' possibile chiamare direttamente all'estero?
	Ay posseebeelay keeahmahray deerayttahmayntay ahllaystayro?
Do I have to go through the switchboard?	Bisogna chiamare tramite il centralino?
	Beezoneeah keeahmahray trahmeetay eel chayntrahleeno?
Do I have to dial _____ '0' first?	Bisogna prima fare lo zero?
	Beezoneeah preemah fahray lo dzayro?
Do I have to book _____ my calls?	Bisogna prenotare la telefonata?
	Beezoneeah praynotahray lah taylayfonahtah?

La vogliono al telefono	There's a phone call for you
Bisogna prima fare lo zero	You have to dial '0' first
Un attimo per favore	One moment, please
Non risponde nessuno	There's no answer
Il numero è occupato	The line's engaged
Vuole aspettare?	Do you want to hold?
Le passo...	Putting you through
Ha sbagliato numero	You've got a wrong number
In questo momento non c'è	He's/she's not here right now
Tornerà alle...	He'll/she'll be back at...
Questa è la segreteria telefonica di...	This is the answering machine of...

Could you dial this ____ number for me, please?	Mi potrebbe fare il seguente numero per favore?
	Mee potraybbay fahray eel saygwayntay noomayro payr fahvoray?
Could you put me ____ through to.../ extension..., please?	Mi potrebbe passare.../interno numero...per favore?
	Mee potraybbay pahssahray.../eentayrno noomayro...payr fahvoray?
I'd like to place a ____ reverse charge call to...	Vorrei fare una telefonata a carico del destinatario, numero...
	Vorrayee fahray oonah taylayfonahtah ah kahreeko dayl daysteenahtahreeo, noomayro...
What's the charge per ____ minute?	Quanto costa al minuto?
	Kwahnto kostah ahl meenooto?
Have there been any ____ calls for me?	C'è stata una chiamata per me?
	Chay stahtah oonah keeahmahtah payr may?

The conversation

Hello, this is... _____	Pronto, sono...
	Pronto, sono...
Who is this, please? ____	Chi parla?
	Kee pahrlah?
Is this...? _____	Parlo con...?
	Pahrlo kon...?
I'm sorry, I've dialled ____ the wrong number	Scusi, ho sbagliato numero
	Skoozee, o zbahllyahto noomayro
I can't hear you_____	Non La sento
	Non lah saynto
I'd like to speak to... ____	Vorrei parlare con...
	Vorrayee pahrlahray kon...
Is there anybody_____ who speaks English?	C'è qualcuno che parla inglese?
	Chay kwahlkoono kay pahrlah eenglaysay?
Extension..., please ____	Mi passi l'interno numero...
	Mee pahssee leentayrno noomayro...

Could you ask him/her to call me back?	Potrebbe chiedergli/chiederle di richiamarmi?
	Potraybbay keeaydayrlly/keeaydayrlay dee reekeeahmahrmee?
My name's... My number's...	Il mio nome è...Il mio numero è...
	Eel meeo nomay ay...Eel meeo noomayro ay...
Could you tell him/her I called?	Gli/le dica che ho chiamato
	Lly/lay deekah kay o keeahmahto
I'll call him/her back tomorrow	Lo/la richiamerò domani
	Lo/lah reekyahmayro domahnee

10 Shopping

● **Shops** are generally open Mon–Sat 9–1 and 3.30–7.30 or 4–8. Grocery shops could stay open until 9pm in summer. Department stores, shops and supermarkets close for a half day during the week.

10.1 Shopping conversations

Where can I get...?	**Dove posso comprare...?** *Dovay posso komprahray...?*
When is this shop open?	**Quando è aperto questo negozio?** *Kwahndo ay ahpayrto kwaysto naygotzeeo?*
Could you tell me where the...department is?	**Mi potrebbe indicare il reparto...?** *Mee potraybbay eendeekahray eel raypahrto...?*
Could you help me, please? I'm looking for...	**Mi potrebbe aiutare? Cerco...** *Mee potraybbay aeeootahray? Chayrko...*
Do you sell English/ American newspapers?	**Vende dei giornali inglesi/americani?** *Venday dayee jornahlee eenglaysee/ahmayreekahnee?*

La stanno servendo?   Are you being served?

No, I'd like...	**No. Vorrei...** *No. Vorrayee...*
I'm just looking, if that's all right	**Sto solo guardando** *Sto solo gwahrdahndo*

(Desidera) altro?   (Would you like) anything else?

Yes, I'd also like...	**Sì, mi dia anche...** *See, mee deeah ahnkay...*

alimentari grocery shop

barbiere barber's

calzature footwear

cartoleria stationery shop

casalinghi household goods

edicola news-stand

enoteca stock of vintage wines

erboristeria herbalist's shop

farmacia pharmacy

fioraio florist

forno/fornaio bakery

fruttivendolo green grocer

gelateria icecream shop

gioielleria jeweller

grande magazzino department store

istituto di bellezza beauty salon

latteria dairy (shop selling dairy products)

lavanderia laundry

lavanderia a gettone/a secco coin-operated laundry/dry cleaner

libreria book shop

macelleria butcher's shop

riparazione moto/biciclette motorbike and bicycle repairs

mercato market

merceria haberdashery

negozio dell'usato second-hand shop

negozio di abbigliamento clothing shop

negozio di articoli da campeggio camping supplies shop

negozio di articoli di fotografia camera shop

negozio di articoli sportivi sporting goods

negozio di dischi music shop (CDs, tapes etc)

negozio di elettrodomestici household (white) goods

negozio di frutta e verdura/ fruttivendolo fruit and vegetable shop

negozio di giocattoli toy shop

negozio di strumenti musicali musical instrument shop

negozio fai-da-te DIY shop

oreficeria goldsmith

orologeria watches and clocks

ottico optician

panetteria baker's shop

parrucchiere hairdresser

pasticceria confectioner's/cake shop

pelletteria leather goods

pellicceria furrier

pescivendolo/ pescheria fishmonger

polleria poultry shop

profumeria perfumery

salumeria delicatessen

supermercato supermarket

tabacchi tobacconist

vivaio nursery (plants)

No, thank you. _____ That's all	No grazie, basta così *No grahtzeeay, bahstah cozee*
Could you show me...?_	Mi potrebbe far vedere...? *Mee potraybbay fahr vaydayray...?*
I'd prefer... _____	Preferisco... *Prayfayreesko...*
This is not what I'm ____ looking for	Non è quello che cerco *Non ay kwayllo kay chayrko*
Thank you. I'll keep ____ looking	Grazie. Proverò da qualche altra parte *Grahtzeeay. Provayro dah kwahlkay ahltrah pahrtay*
Do you have _____ something...?	Ha qualcosa di...? *Ah kwahlkosah dee...?*
– less expensive?_____	Ha qualcosa di meno caro? *Ah kwahlkosah dee mayno kahro?*
– smaller? _____	Ha qualcosa di più piccolo? *Ah kwahlkosah dee peeoo peekkolo?*
– larger? _____	Ha qualcosa di più grande? *Ah kwahlkosah dee peeoo grahnday?*
I'll take this one _____	Prendo questo/a qui *Prayndo kwaysto/ah kwee*
Does it come with ____ instructions?	Ci sono le istruzioni per l'uso? *Chee sono lay eestrootzeeonee payr loozo?*
It's too expensive_____	E' troppo caro *Ay troppo kahro*
I'll give you... _____	Le posso dare... *Lay posso dahray...*
Could you keep this ____ for me? I'll come back for it later	Me lo potrebbe tenere da parte? Verrò a prenderlo più tardi *May lo potraybbay taynayray dah pahrtay? Vayrro ah prayndayrlo peeoo tahrdee*
Do you have a bag? ____ for me, please?	Ha un sacchetto? *Ah oon sahkkaytto?*
Could you giftwrap ____ it, please?	Mi potrebbe fare una confezione regalo, per favore? *Mee potraybbay fahray oonah konfaytzeeonay raygahlo, payr fahvoray?*

Mi dispiace, questo non ce l'abbiamo	I'm sorry, we don't have that.
Mi dispiace, sono finiti/e	I'm sorry, we're sold out.
Mi dispiace, arriverà solo tra...	I'm sorry, it won't come back in until....
Paghi alla cassa	Please pay at the cash desk
Non accettiamo carte di credito	We don't accept credit cards.
Non accettiamo traveller cheques	We don't accept traveller's cheques.
Non accettiamo valuta straniera	We don't accept foreign currency.

10.2 Food

I'd like a hundred _____ grams of..., please	Vorrei un etto di... *Vorrayee oon aytto dee...*
I'd like half a kilo/five___ hundred grams of...	Vorrei mezzo chilo/cinquecento grammi di... *Vorrayee maydzo keelo/cheenkwaychaynto grahmmee dee...*
I'd like a kilo of... _____	Vorrei un chilo di... *Vorrayee oon keelo dee...*
Could you...it for me,___ please?	Me lo potrebbe...? *May lo potraybbay...?*
– slice it/cut it up for ___ me, please?	Me lo potrebbe affettare/tagliare a pezzi? *May lo potraybbay ahffayttahray/tahllyahray ah paytzee?*
– grate it for me, _____ please?	Me lo potrebbe grattugiare? *May lo potraybbay grahttoojahray?*
Can I order it?_____	Potrei ordinarlo? *Potrayee ordeenahrlo?*
I'll pick it up tomorrow/_ at...	Verrò a prenderlo domani/alle... *Vayrro ah prayndayrlo domahny/ahllay...*

Can you eat/drink this?	Si può mangiare/bere questo?
	See pwo mahnjahray/bayhray kwaysto?
What's in it?	Cosa c'è dentro?
	Kosah chay dayntro?

10.3 Clothing and shoes

I saw something in the window. Shall I point it out?	Ho visto qualcosa in vetrina. Vuole che glielo indichi?
	O veesto kwahlkosah een vaytreenah. Vwolay kay lyeeaylo eendeekee?
I'd like something to go with this	Vorrei qualcosa che vada bene con questo/a
	Vorrayee kwahlkosah kay vahdah behnay kon kwaysto/ah
Do you have shoes to match this?	Ha delle scarpe nello stesso colore di questo/a?
	Ah dayllay skahrpay nayllo staysso koloray dee kwaysto/ah?
I'm a size...in the UK	In Inghilterra la mia misura è...
	Een Eengeeltayrrah lah meeah meezoorah ay...
Can I try this on?	Posso provarlo/provarla?
	Posso provahrlo/provahrlah?
Where's the fitting room?	Dov'è il camerino?
	Dovay ay eel kahmayreeno?
It doesn't suit me	Non mi sta bene
	Non mee stah bayhnay
This is the right size	Questa è la misura giusta
	Kwaystah ay lah meezoorah joostah
It doesn't look good on me	Mi sta male
	Mee stah mahlay
Do you have this/ these in...?	Ha questo(a)/questi(e) in...?
	Ah kwaysto(ah)/kwaystee(ay) een...?

Bucato a mano	Lavaggio a secco	Non stirare
Hand wash	Dry clean	Do not iron
Bucato in lavatrice	Non centrifugare	Stendere piatto
Machine washable	Do not spin dry	Lay flat

The heel's too high/low	Il tacco è troppo alto/basso
	Eel tahkko ay troppo ahlto/bahsso
Is this real leather?	E' pelle vera?
	Ay payllay vayhrah?
Is this genuine hide?	E' vero cuoio?
	Ay vayhro kwoeeo?
I'm looking for a...for a...year-old child	Cerco un/una...per un bambino/una bambina di...anni
	Chayrko oon/oonah...payr oon bahmbeeno/oonah bahmbeenah dee...ahnnee
I'd like a...	Vorrei un/una...di...
	Vorrayee oon/oonah...dee...
– silk	Vorrei un/una...di seta
	Vorrayee oon/oonah...dee saytah
– cotton	Vorrei un/una...di cotone
	Vorrayee oon/oonah...dee kotonay
– woollen	Vorrei un/una...di lana
	Vorrayee oon/oonah...dee lahnah
– linen	Vorrei un/una...di lino
	Vorrayee oon/oonah...dee leeno
At what temperature should I wash it?	A che temperatura va lavato/a?
	Ah kay taympayrahtoorah vah lahvahto/ah?
Will it shrink in the wash?	Si restringe con il lavaggio?
	See raystreenjay kon eel lahvahdjo?

At the cobbler

| Could you mend these shoes? | Mi può riparare queste scarpe? |
| | *Mee pwo reepahrahray kwaystay skahrpay?* |

Could you resole/ reheel these shoes?	Potrebbe risuolare queste scarpe/rifare i tacchi a queste scarpe?
	Potraybbay reeswolahray kwaystay skahrpay/reefahray ee tahkkee ah kwaystay skahrpay?
When will they be ready?	Quando saranno pronte?
	Kwahndo sahrahnno prontay?
I'd like..., please	Vorrei...
	Vorrayee...
– a tin of shoe polish	Vorrei una scatola di lucido da scarpe
	Vorrayee oonah skahtolah dee loocheedo dah skahrpay
– a pair of shoelaces	Vorrei un paio di lacci
	Vorrayee oon paheeo dee lahtchee

10.4 Photographs and video

I'd like a film for this camera, please	Vorrei una pellicola per questa macchina fotografica
	Vorrayee oonah paylleekolah payr kwaystah mahkkeenah fotograhfeekah
I'd like a cartridge, please	Vorrei una cassetta
	Vorrayee oonah kahssayttah
– a one twenty-six cartridge	Vorrei una cassetta centoventisei
	Vorrayee oonah kahssayttah chayntovaynteesay
– a slide film	Vorrei una pellicola diapositive
	Vorrayee oonah paylleekolah deeahposeeteevay
– a movie cassette, please	Vorrei una cassetta per cinepresa
	Vorrayee oonah kahssayttah payr cheenaypraysah
– a videotape	Vorrei una cassetta per videoregistrazione
	Vorrayee oonah kahssayttah payr veedayo-rayjeestrahtzeeonay

– colour/black and white	– a colori/bianco e nero
	– ah koloree/beeahnko ay nayhro
– super eight	– super otto
	– soopayr otto
– 12/24/36 exposures	– dodici/ventiquattro/trentasei pose
	– dodeechee/vaynteekwahttro/ trayntahsayèe posay
– ASA/DIN number	– numero ASA/DIN
	– noomayro ASA/DEEN

Problems

Could you load the film for me, please?	Potrebbe mettermi il rullino nella macchina fotografica?
	Potraybbay mayttayrmee eel roolleeno nellah mahkkeenah fotograhfeekah?
Could you take the film out for me, please?	Potrebbe levare la pellicola dalla macchina fotografica?
	Potraybbay layvahray lah paylleekolah dahllah mahkkeenah fotograhfeekah?
Should I replace the batteries?	Devo cambiare le pile?
	Dayvo kahmbyahray lay peelay?
Could you have a look at my camera, please? It's not working	Potrebbe controllare la mia macchina fotografica? Non funziona più
	Potraybbay kontrollahray lah meeah mahkkeenah fotograhfeekah? Non foontzeeonah peeoo
The...is broken	....è guasto/a
	....ay gwahsto/ah
The film's jammed	La pellicola si è bloccata
	Lah paylleekolah see ay blokkahtah
The film's broken	La pellicola si è rotta
	Lah paylleekolah see ay rottah
The flash isn't working	Il flash non funziona
	Eel flash non foontzeeonah

Processing and prints

I'd like to have this film_ developed/printed, please	Vorrei far sviluppare/far stampare questa pellicola *Vorrayee fahr sveelooppahray/fahr stahmpahray kwaystah paylleekolah*
I'd like...prints from ____ each negative	Vorrei...copie di ogni negativo *Vorrayee...copeeay dee onyee naygahteevo*
glossy/mat_____	lucido/opaco *loocheedo/opahko*
6x9 _____	sei per nove *sayee payr novay*
I'd like to order reprints_ of these photos	Vorrei far fare un'altra ristampa di queste foto *Vorrayee fahr fahray oonahltrah reestahmpah dee kwaystay foto*
I'd like to have this_____ photo enlarged	Vorrei far ingrandire questa foto *Vorrayee fahr eengrahndeeray kwaystah foto*
How much is_____ processing?	Quanto costa lo sviluppo? *Kwahnto kostah lo sveelooppo?*
How much for _____ printing?	Quanto costa la stampa? *Kwahnto kostah lah stahmpah?*
How much is are the ___ reprints?	Quanto costa la ristampa? *Kwahnto kostah lah reestahmpah?*
How much is it for _____ enlargement?	Quanto costa l'ingrandimento? *Kwahnto kostah leengrahndeemaynto?*
When will they _____ be ready?	Quando saranno pronte? *Kwahndo sahrahnno prontay?*

10.5 At the hairdresser's

Do I have to make an __ appointment?	Bisogna prendere un appuntamento?
	Beezoneeah prayndayray oon ahppoontahmaynto?
Can I come in straight __ away?	E' subito a mia disposizione?
	Ay soobeeto ah meeah deesposeetzeeonay?
How long will I have ___ to wait?	Quanto devo aspettare?
	Kwahnto dayvo ahspayttahray?
I'd like a shampoo/ ____ haircut	Vorrei farmi lavare/tagliare i capelli
	Vorrayèe fahrmee lahvahray/tahllyahray ee kahpayllee
I'd like a shampoo for __ oily/dry hair, please	Vorrei uno shampoo per capelli grassi/secchi
	Vorrayee oono shahmpo payr kahpayllee grahssy/saykkee
I'd like an anti-dandruff_ shampoo	Vorrei uno shampoo anti-forfora
	Vorrayee oono shahmpo ahnteeforforah
I'd like a colour-rinse ___ shampoo, please	Vorrei uno shampoo colorante
	Vorrayee oono shahmpo kolorahntay
I'd like a shampoo with_ conditioner, please	Vorrei uno shampoo con balsamo
	Vorrayee oono shahmpo kon bahlsahmo
I'd like highlights, _____ please	Vorrei i colpi di sole
	Vorrayee ee kolpee dee solay
Do you have a colour __ chart, please?	Ha una tabella dei colori, per favore?
	Ah oonah tahbayllah dayèe koloree, payr fahvoray?
I'd like to keep the ____ same colour	Non vorrei cambiare colore
	Non vorrayee kahmbeeahray koloray
I'd like it darker/lighter _	Li vorrei più scuri/più chiari
	Lee vorrayee peeoo skooree/peeoo keeahree
I'd like/I don't want ____ hairspray	Vorrei/Non voglio la lacca
	Vorrayee/Non vollyo lah lahkkah

– gel _____	– il gel
	– *eel jayl*
– lotion _____	– la lozione
	– *lah lotzeeonay*
I'd like a short fringe ___	Vorrei una frangetta corta
	Vorrayee oonah frahnjayttah kortah
Not too short at the ___ back	Non troppo corti dietro
	Non troppo kortee deeayhtro
Not too long _____	Non troppo lunghi
	Non troppo loongee
I'd like it curly/not _____ too curly	Li vorrei ricci/non troppo ricci
	Lee vorrayee reetchee/non troppo reetchee
It needs a little/_____ a lot taken off	Me li tagli un po' più corti/molto più corti
	May lee tahlly oon po peeoo kortee/molto peeoo kortee
I'd like a completely____ different style/a different cut	Vorrei cambiare pettinatura/un taglio diverso
	Vorrayee kahmbyahray paytteenahtoorah/oon tahleeo deevayrso
I'd like it the same as __ in this photo	Vorrei un taglio come in questa foto
	Vorrayèe oon tahllyo komay een kwaystah foto
– as that lady's _____	– come quella signora
	– *komay kwayllah seeneeorah*
Could you put the _____ drier up/down a bit?	Può alzare/abbassare un po'il casco?
	Pwo ahltzahray/ahbbahssahray oon po eel kahsko?
I'd like a facial_____	Vorrei una maschera per il viso
	Vorrayee oonah mahskayhra payr eel veezo
– a manicure _____	la manicure
	– *lah mahneekooray*
– a massage _____	– un massaggio
	– *oon mahssahdjo*
Could you trim my..., ___ please?	Vorrei che mi desse una spuntatina
	Vorrayee kay mee dayssay oonah spoontahteenah

Come desidera che siano tagliati i capelli?	How do you want it cut?
Quale taglio ha in mente?	What style did you have in mind?
Quale colore desidera?	What colour did you want it?
Le va bene la temperatura?	Is the temperature all right for you?
Desidera leggere qualcosa?	Would you like something to read?
Desidera bere qualcosa?	Would you like a drink?
Le va bene così?	Is this what you had in mind?

– fringe? _____ – alla frangetta
– ahllah frahnjayttah

– beard?_____ – alla barba
– ahllah bahrbah

– moustache? _____ – ai baffi
– ahee bahffee

I'd like a shave, please _ Mi faccia la barba, per favore
Mee fahtchah lah bahrbah, payr fahvoray

I'd like a wet shave, ____ Vorrei essere raso con la lametta
 please *Vorray ayssayray rahzo kon lah lahmayttah*

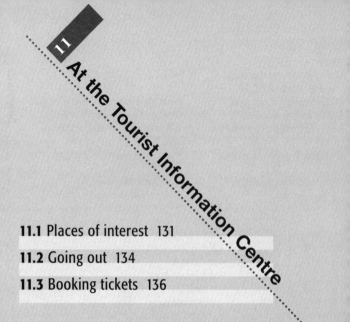

11

At the Tourist Information Centre

11.1 Places of interest

●**There are three main categories** of tourist office: regional, provincial and local. Regional offices are mainly concerned with planning and budgeting etc. Provincial offices (EPT or APT) usually have information on regions and towns. A good range of more specific local information about buses, museums, tours etc. is available at CIT and AAST offices. Tourist offices are generally open Monday to Friday, 8.30am to 12 or 1pm and 3pm to 7pm. Some also open on Saturdays and Sundays during the summer.

Where's the Tourist Information, please?	Senta, dov'è l'ufficio informazioni turistiche?
	Sayntah, dovay ay looffeetcheeo eenformahtzeeonee tooreesteekay?
Do you have a city map?	Ha una piantina della città, per favore?
	Ah oonah peeahnteenah dayllah cheettah, pahr fahvoray?
Where is the museum?	Dov`è il museo?
	Dovay ay eel moosayo?
Where can I find a church?	Dove posso trovare una chiesa?
	Dovay posso trovahray oonah keeaysah?
Could you give me some information about...?	Mi potrebbe dare qualche informazione su...?
	Mee potraybbay dahray kwahlkay eenformahtzeeonay soo...?
How much is this?	Quanto costa?
	Kwahnto kostah?
What are the main places of interest?	Quali sono i monumenti più interessanti da vedere?
	Kwahlee sono ee monoomayntee peeoo eentayrayssahntee dah vaydayray?
Could you point them out on the map?	Me li potrebbe indicare sulla pianta?
	May lee potraybbay eendeekahray soollah pyahntah?

What do you _____ recommend?	Cosa ci consiglia?
	Kosah chee konseellyah?
We'll be here for a _____ few hours	Ci fermeremo qui per qualche ora
	Chee fayrmayraymo kwee payr kwahlkay orah
We'll be here for a day _	Ci fermeremo qui per un giorno
	Chee fayrmayraymo kwee payr oon jorno
We'll be here for a _____ week	Ci fermeremo qui per una settimana
	Chee fayrmayraymo kwee payr oonah saytteemahnah
We're interested in... ___	Siamo interessati a...
	Seeahmo eentayhrayssahtee ah...
Is there a scenic walk __ around the city?	E' possibile seguire un itinerario turistico della città?
	Ay posseebeelay saygweeray oon eeteenayrahreeo tooreesteeko dayllah cheettah?
How long does it take?_	Quanto dura?
	Kwahnto doorah?
Where does it _____ start/end?	Dove comincia/finisce?
	Dovay komeenchah/feeneeshay?
Are there any boat _____ trips?	E' possibile fare un giro in battello?
	Ay posseebeelay fahray oon jeero een bahttayllo?
Where can we board?__	Dove possiamo imbarcarci?
	Dovay posseeahmo eembahrkahrchee?
Are there any coach ___ tours?	E' possibile fare un giro della città in pullman?
	Ay posseebeelay fahray oon jeero dayllah cheettah een poollmahn?
Where do we get on? __	Dove possiamo salire?
	Dovay posseeahmo sahleeray?
Is there a guide who ___ speaks English?	C'è una guida che parla inglese?
	Chay oonah gweedah kay pahrla englaysay?

What trips can we take around the area?	Quali gite si possono fare nei dintorni?
	Kwahlee jeetay see possono fahray nayee deentornee?
Are there any excursions?	Ci sono delle escursioni?
	Chee sono dayllay ayskoorseeonee?
Where do they go?	Dove vanno?
	Dovay vahnno?
We'd like to go to...	Vogliamo andare a...
	Vollyahmo ahndahray ah...
How long is the excursion?	Quanto tempo dura l'escursione?
	Kwahnto taympo doorah layskoorseeonay?
How long do we stay in...?	Per quanto tempo ci fermeremo a...?
	Payr kwahnto taympo chee fayrmayraymo ah...?
Are there any guided tours?	Ci sono delle visite guidate?
	Chee sono dayllay veeseetay gweedahtay?
How much free time will we have there?	Quanto tempo libero avremo a disposizione?
	Kwahnto taympo leebayro ahvraymo ah deesposeetzeeonay?
We want to have a walk around/to go on foot	Vogliamo fare un giro a piedi
	Vollyahmo fahray oon jeero ah peeaydee
Can we hire a guide?	E' possibile avere una guida?
	Ay posseebeelay ahvayray oonah gweedah?
Can we book an alpine hut?	E' possibile prenotare dei rifugi alpini?
	Ay pooseebeelay praynotahray dayee reefoojee ahlpeenee?
What time does... open/close?	A che ora apre/chiude...?
	Ah kay orah ahpray/keeooday...?
What days is...open/ closed?	Quali sono i giorni in cui...è aperto/a/chiuso/a?
	Kwahlee sono ee jornee een kooee...ay ahpyrto/ah keeoozo/ah?
What's the admission price?	Quanto costa un biglietto d'ingresso?
	Kwahnto kostah oon beellyaytto deengraysso?

Is there a group _____ discount?	C'è uno sconto per gruppi? *Chay oono skonto payr grooppee?*
Is there a child _____ discount?	C'è uno sconto per bambini? *Chay oono skonto payr bahmbeenee?*
Is there a discount for __ pensioners/senior citizens?	C'è uno sconto per anziani? *Chay oono skonto payr ahntzeeahnee?*
Can I take (flash) _____ photos/can I film here?	Qui è permesso fotografare (con il flash)/filmare? *Kwee ay payrmaysso fotograhfahray (kon eel flash)/feelmahray?*
Do you have any _____ postcards of...?	Avete cartoline di...? *Avaytay kahrtoleenay dee...?*
Do you have an _____ English...?	Ha un/una...in inglese? *Ah oon/oonah...een eenglaysay?*
– catalogue? _____	– catalogo? *– kahtahlogo?*
– programme? _____	– programma? *– prograhmmah?*
– brochure? _____	– opuscolo? *– opooskolo?*

11.2 Going out

● **The main theatre season** is during the winter. Classical music concerts are performed throughout the year. Florence offers the *Maggio Musicale Fiorentino*, *La Scala* is Milan's famous opera house and *Umbria Jazz* takes place in *Perugia* in July. There is a very popular Italian film industry and most foreign films are dubbed into Italian. Venice offers an international film festival and the *Biennale*, a visual arts festival held every two years.

Do you have this ___ week's/month's entertainment guide?	Ha il calendario delle manifestazioni e degli spettacoli di questa settimana/di questo mese?
	Ah eel kahlayndahreeo dayllay mahneefaystatzeeonee ay daylly spayttahkkolee dee kwaystah saytteemahnah/dee kwaysto maysay?
What's on tonight? ___	Che spettacoli ci sono stasera?
	Kay spayttahkolee chee sono stahsayhrah?
We want to go to... ___	Vorremmo andare a...
	Vorraymmo ahndahray ah...
What's on at the ___ cinema?	Che film danno al cinema?
	Kay feelm dahnno ahl cheenaymah?
What sort of film is ___ that?	Che tipo di film è?
	Kay teepo dee feelm ay?
– suitable for everyone ___	– per tutti
	– payr toottee
– not suitable for under ___ 12s/under 16s	– vietato ai minori di dodici/sedici anni
	– veeaytahto ayee meenoree dee dodeechee/saydeechee ahnnee
– original version ___	– versione originale
	– vayrseeonay oreejeenahlay
– subtitled ___	– con sottotitoli
	– kon sottoteetolee
– dubbed ___	– doppiato
	– doppeeahto
Is it a continuous ___ showing?	E' uno spettacolo continuato?
	Ay oono spayttahkolo konteenooahto?
What's on at...? ___	Che danno a...?
	Kay dahnno ah...?
– the theatre? ___	– al teatro?
	– ahl tayahtro?
– the opera? ___	– al teatro lirico?
	– ahl tayahtro leereeko?
What's happening in the concert hall?	Quale concerto danno al teatro?
	Kwahlay konchayrto dahnno ahl tayahtro?

Where can I find a ____ good disco around here?	C'è una buona discoteca qui vicino?
	Chay oonah bwonah deeskotaykah kwee veecheeno?
Is it members only? ____	E' richiesta la tessera?
	Ay reekeeaystah lah tayssayrah?
Where can I find a good nightclub around here?	C'è un buon night qui vicino?
	Chay oon bwon neeght kwee veecheeno?
Is it evening wear only?	E' obbligatorio l'abito da sera?
	Ay obbleegahtoreeo lahbeeto dah sayhrah?
Should I/we dress up? _	E' necessario un abito elegante?
	Ay naychayssahreeo oon ahbeeto aylaygahntay?
What time does the ____ show start?	A che ora comincia lo show?
	Ah kay orah komeenchah lo show?
When's the next _____ soccer match?	Quando è la prossima partita di calcio?
	Kwahndo ay lah prosseemah pahrteetah dee kahlcho?
Who's playing? _____	Chi gioca?
	Kee jokah?
I'd like an escort (m/f) _ for tonight	Stasera vorrei un accompagnatore/un'accompagnatrice
	Stahsayhrah vorrayèe oon ahkkompahneeahtroray/oonahkkompahne eatreechay

11.3 Booking tickets

Could you book some___ tickets for us?	Ci potrebbe fare la prenotazione, per favore?
	Chee potraybbay fahray lah praynotatzeeonay payr fahvoray?
We'd like to book... ____ seats/a table for...	Vogliamo...posti/un tavolo per...
	Vollyahmo...postee/oon tahvolo payr...

– seats in the stalls in __ the main section	Vogliamo...poltrone in platea in sala *Vollyahmo...poltronay een plahtayah een sahlah*
– seats in the circle ____	Vogliamo...posti in galleria *Vollyahmo...postee een gahllayryah*
– a box for... _____	Vogliamo un palco con...posti *Vollyahmo oon pahlko kon...postee*
– front row seats/a ____ table for...at the front	Vogliamo...posti/un tavolo per...nelle prime file *Vollyahmo...postee/oon tahvolo payr...nayllay preemay feelay*

Per quale spettacolo vuole fare una prenotazione?	Which performance do you want to book for?
Che tipo di posto?	Where would you like to sit?
E' tutto esaurito	Everything's sold out
Sono rimasti solo posti in piedi	It's standing room only
Sono rimasti solo posti in galleria	We've only got circle seats left
Sono rimasti solo posti in loggione	We've only got upper circle (in the gods) seats left
Sono rimaste solo le poltrone in platea	We've only got stalls seats left
Sono rimasti solo posti nelle prime file	We've only got front row seats left
Sono rimasti solo i posti in fondo	We've only got seats left at the back
Quanti posti desidera?	How many seats would you like?
Deve ritirare i biglietti prima delle...	You'll have to pick up the tickets before...o'clock
Biglietti prego	Tickets, please
Ecco il suo posto	This is your seat
Siete seduti nel posto sbagliato	You are in the wrong seat

...seats in the middle/a table in the middle	Vogliamo...posti/un tavolo al centro *Vollyahmo...postee/oon tahvolo ahl chayntro*
...back row seats/a table at the back	Vogliamo...posti/un tavolo in fondo *Vollyahmo...postee/oon tahvolo een fondo*
Could I book...seats for the...o'clock performance?	E' possibile prenotare...posti per lo spettacolo delle...? *Ay posseebeelay praynotahray...postee payr lo spayttahkolo dayllay...?*
Are there any seats left for tonight?	Ci sono ancora biglietti per stasera? *Chee sono ahnkorah beellyayttee payr stahsayhrah?*
How much is a ticket?	Quanto costa un biglietto? *Kwahnto kostah oon beellyaytto?*
When can I pick up the tickets?	Quando posso ritirare i biglietti? *Kwahndo posso reeteerahray ee beellyayttee?*
I've got a reservation	Ho prenotato *O praynotahto*
My name's... _____	Il mio nome è... *eel meeo nomay ay...*

12.1 Sporting questions

Where can we... _____ around here?	Dove possiamo...qui vicino? *Dovay posseeahmo...kwee veecheeno?*
Can I/we hire a...? _____	E' possibile prendere a nolo un/una...? *Ay posseebeelay praydayray ah nolo oon/oonah...?*
Can I/we _____ take...lessons?	E' possibile prendere lezioni di...? *Ay posseebeelay prendayray laytzeeonee dee...?*
How much is that per ___ hour/per day/How much is each one?	Quanto costa all'ora/al giorno/a lezione? *Kwahnto kostah ahllorah/ahl jorno/ah laytzeeonay?*
Do you need a permit ___ for that?	Bisogna avere una licenza? *Beezoneeah ahvayray oonah leechaynzah?*
Where can I get _____ the permit?	Dove posso ottenere questa licenza? *Dovay posso ottaynayray kwaystah leechaynzah?*

12.2 By the waterfront

Is it far (to walk) to _____ the sea?	Per andare al mare, c'è molto (a piedi)? *Payr ahndahray ahl mahray chay molto (ah peeaydee)?*
Is there a...around _____ here?	C'è un/una...qui vicino? *Chay oon/oonah...kwee veecheeno?*
– a swimming pool_____	C'è una piscina? *Chay oonah peesheenah?*
– a sandy beach_____	C'è una spiaggia di sabbia? *Chay oonah speeahdjah dee sahbbeeah?*
– a nudist beach_____	C'è una spiaggia per nudisti? *Chay oonah speeahdjah payr noodeestee?*
– mooring (place)/dock _	C'è un molo d'attracco? *Chay oon molo dahttrahkko?*
Are there any rocks _____ here?	Ci sono degli scogli qui? *Chee sono daylly skolly kwee?*

Zona di pesca	Divieto di	Pesca vietata
Fishing waters	balneazione	No fishing
Pericolo Danger	No swimming	
Solo con licenza	Divieto di surfing	
Permits only	No surfing	

When's high/low tide? __	Quando c'è l'alta marea/la bassa marea?
	Kwahndo chay lahltah mahrayah/lah bahssah mahrayah?
What's the water _____ temperature?	Qual è la temperatura dell'acqua?
	Kwahlay ay lah taympayrahtoorah dayllahkwah?
Is it (very) deep here? __	E' (molto) profondo qui?
	Ay (molto) profondo kwee?
Is it safe (for children) __ to swim here?	E' sicuro (per i bambini) fare il bagno qui?
	Ay seekooro (payr ee bahmbeenee) fahray eel bahneeo kwee?
Are there any currents?_	Ci sono correnti?
	Chee sono korrayntee?
Are there any rapids/____ waterfalls along this river?	Questo fiume ha delle rapide/delle cascate?
	Kwaysto feeoomay ah dayllay rahpeeday/kahskahtay?
What does that flag/ ____ buoy mean?	Cosa significa quella bandiera/quella boa?
	Kosah seeneefeekah kwayllah bahndeeayrah/kwayllah boah?
Is there a lifeguard on __ duty?	C'è un bagnino che sorveglia?
	Chay oon bahneeno kay sorvellyah?
Are dogs allowed _____ here?	Sono permessi i cani?
	Sono payrmayssee ee kahnee?
Is camping on the _____ beach allowed?	E' permesso fare il campeggio sulla spiaggia?
	Ay payrmaysso fahray eel kahmpaydjo soollah speeahdjah?
Can we light a fire? ____	E' permesso fare un fuoco?
	Ay payrmaysso fahray oon fwoko?

12.3 In the snow

Can I take ski lessons __ here?	E' possibile prendere delle lezioni di sci?
	Ay posseebeelay prayndayray dayllay laytzeeonee dee shee?
For beginners/ _____ intermediates	Per principianti/di medio livello
	Payr preencheepeeahntee/dee maydeeo leevello
How large are the_____ groups?	Quanti persone ci sono in un gruppo?
	Kwahntay payrsonay chee sono een oon grooppo?
What languages are____ the classes in?	In che lingua fanno lezione?
	Een kay leengwah fahnno laytzeeonay?
I'd like a lift pass, _____ please	Vorrei uno skipass
	Vorrayee oono skeepahss
Where are the nursery __ slopes?	Dove sono le piste per i principianti?
	Dovay sono lay peestay payr ee preencheepeeahntee?
Are there any_____ cross-country ski runs around here?	Ci sono piste di fondo qui vicino?
	Chee sono peestay dee fondo kwee veecheeno?
Have the cross-country runs been marked?	Sono indicate le piste di fondo?
	Sono eendeekahtay lay peestay dee fondo?
Are the...open? _____	Sono aperti...i/le?
	Sono ahpayrtee...ee/lay?
– the ski lifts...? _____	Sono aperti gli skilift?
	Sono ahpayrtee lly skeeleeft?
– the chair lifts...?_____	Sono aperte le seggiovie?
	Sono ahpayrtee lay sedgeeoveeay
– the runs...? _____	Sono aperte le piste?
	Sono ahpayrtee lay peestay?
– the cross-country ____ runs...?	Sono aperte le piste di fondo?
	Sono ahpayrtay lay peestay dee fondo?

13

Sickness

13.1 Call (fetch) the doctor

● **If you become ill** or need emergency treatment, it is better to go to Casualty (*pronto soccorso*) at your nearest hospital.

Could you call (fetch) a doctor quickly, please?	Mi chiami presto il medico, per favore *Mee keeahmy praysto eel maydeeko, payr fahvoray*
When does the doctor have surgery?	Quando riceve il medico? *Kwahndo reechayvay eel maydeeko?*
When can the doctor come?	Quando potrà venire il medico? *Kwahndo potrah vayneeray eel maydeeko?*
Could I make an appointment to see the doctor?	Mi potrebbe fissare un appuntamento con il medico? *Mee potraybbay feessahray oon ahppoontahmaynto con eel maydeeko?*
I've got an appointment to see the doctor at... o'clock	Ho un appuntamento con il medico alle... *O oon ahppoontahmaynto con eel maydeeko ahllay...*
Which doctor/ pharmacy is on night/weekend duty?	Quale medico/farmacia è in servizio notturno/in servizio di fine settimana? *Kwahlay maydeeko/fahrmahcheeah ay een sayrveetzeeo nottoorno/een sayrveetzeeo dee feenay saytteemahnah?*

13.2 Patient's ailments

I don't feel well	Mi sento male *Mee saynto mahlay*
I'm dizzy	Ho il capogiro *O eel kahpojeero*
– ill	Sono ammalato/a *Sono ahmmahlahto/ah*
I feel sick (nauseous)	Ho la nausea *O lah nahoozayah*

I've got a cold_____	Sono raffreddato/a
	Sono rahffrayddahto/ah
It hurts here_____	Mi fa male qui
	Mee fah mahlay kwee
I've been sick	Ho vomitato
(vomited)	*O vomeetahto*
I've got... _____	Soffro di...
	Soffro dee...
I'm running a_____	Ho la febbre...
temperature	*O lah faybbrayah...*
of...degrees	
I've been..._____	Sono stato/a...
	Sono stahto/ah...
– stung by a wasp _____	Sono stato/a punto/a da una vespa
	Sono stahto/ah poonto/ah dah oonah vayspah
– stung by an insect ___	Sono stato/a punto/a da un insetto
	Sono stahto/ah poonto/ah dah oon eensaytto
– bitten by a dog _____	Sono stato/a morso/a da un cane
	Sono stahto/ah morso/ah dah oon kahnay
– stung by a jellyfish ___	Sono stato/a punto/a da una medusa
	Sono stahto/ah poont/ah dah oonah maydoosah
– bitten by a snake ____	Sono stato/a morso/a da una serpe
	Sono stahto/ah morso/ah dah oonah sayrpay
– bitten by an animal___	Sono stato/a morso/a da una bestia
	Sono stahto/ah morso/ah dah oonah baysteeah
I've cut myself _____	Mi sono tagliato/a
	Mee sono tahllyahto/ah
I've burned myself _____	Mi sono bruciato/a
	Mee sono broocheeahto/ah
I've grazed/scratched __	Mi sono scorticato/a, graffiato/a
myself (m/f)	*Mee sono skorteekahto/ah, graffeeahto/ah*

I've had a fall _____	Sono caduto/a
	Sono kahdooto/ah
I've sprained my ankle _	Mi sono storto/a la caviglia
	Mee sono storto/ah lah kahveellyah
I'd like the morning- ___	Vorrei la pillola del giorno dopo
after pill	*Vorrayèe lah peellolah dayl jorno dopo*

13.3 The consultation

Quali disturbi ha?	What seems to be the problem?
Da quanto tempo ha questi disturbi?	How long have you had these complaints?
Ha sofferto già prima di questi disturbi?	Have you had this trouble before?
Ha la febbre? Quanti gradi?	Do you have a temperature? What is it?
Si spogli per favore	Get undressed, please
Si scopra il torace per favore	Strip to the waist, please
Può spogliarsi da questa parte	You can undress there
Si scopra il braccio sinistro/destro per favore	Roll up your left/right sleeve, please
Si sdrai qui, per favore	Lie down here, please
Fa male?	Does this hurt?
Respiri profondamente	Breathe deeply
Apra la bocca	Open your mouth

Patients' medical history

I'm a diabetic _____	Sono diabetico/a
	Sono deeahbayhteeko/ah
I have a heart _____	Soffro di disturbi di cuore
condition	*Soffro dee deestoorbee dee kworay*

I'm an asthmatic_____	Soffro di asma *Soffro dee ahsmah*
I'm allergic to..._____	Sono allergico/a a... *Sono ahllayrjeeko/ah ah...*
I'm...months pregnant__	Sono incinta di...mesi *Sono eencheentah dee...maysee*
I'm on a diet _____	Seguo una dieta *Saygwo oonah deeaytah*
I'm on medication/_____ the pill	Prendo dei farmaci/la pillola contraccettiva *Prayndo dayee fahrmahchee/lah peellolah kontrahchaytteevah*
I've had a heart attack _ once before	Ho avuto già in passato un attacco cardiaco *O ahvooto jah een pahssahto oon ahttahkko kahrdeeahko*
I've had a(n)... _____ operation	Mi hanno fatto un'operazione a... *Mee ahnno fahtto oonopayrahtzeeonay ah...*
I've been ill recently____	Sono stato/a ammalato/a di recente *Sono stahto/ah ahmmahlahto/ah dee raychayntay*
I've got a stomach ____ ulcer	Soffro di un'ulcera gastrica *Soffro dee oonoolchayrah gahstreekah*
I've got my period ____	Ho le mestruazioni *O lay maystrooahtzeeonee*

The diagnosis

E' allergico/a a qualcosa?	Do you have any allergies?
Sta prendendo altri farmaci?	Are you on any medication?
Segue una dieta?	Are you on a diet?
E' incinta?	Are you pregnant?
E' stato/a vaccinato/a contro il tetano?	Have you had a tetanus injection?

Non è niente di grave	It's nothing serious
Ha una frattura al/alla...	Your...is broken
Ha una distorsione al/alla...	You've got a sprained...
Ha uno strappo al/alla...	You've got a torn...
Ha un'infezione	You've got an infection/some inflammation
Ha un'appendicite	You've got appendicitis
Ha una bronchite	You've got bronchitis
Ha una malattia venerea	You've got a venereal disease
Ha l'influenza	You've got the flu
Ha avuto un attacco cardiaco	You've had a heart attack
Ha un'infezione (virale, batterica)	You've got a (viral/bacterial) infection
Ha una polmonite	You've got pneumonia
Ha una gastrite/un'ulcera	You've got gastritis/an ulcer
Ha uno strappo muscolare	You've pulled a muscle
Ha un'infezione vaginale	You've got a vaginal infection
Ha un'intossicazione alimentare	You've got food poisoning
Ha un'insolazione	You've got sunstroke
E' allergico a...	You're allergic to...
E' incinta	You're pregnant
Vorrei fare analizzare il Suo sangue/la Sua orina/le Sue feci	I'd like to have your blood/urine/stools tested
La ferita deve essere suturata	It needs stitches
La indirizzo da uno specialista/ all'ospedale	I'm referring you to a specialist/sending you to hospital.
Bisogna far fare qualche radiografia	You'll need some x-rays taken
Può aspettare un attimo nella sala d'attesa, per favore?	Could you wait in the waiting room, please?
Deve essere operato/a	You'll need an operation

Is it contagious? _____	E' contagioso?
	Ay kontahjozo?
How long do I have to ___ stay...?	Per quanto tempo devo rimanere...?
	Payr kwahnto taympo dayvo reemahnayray...?
– in bed _____	– a letto?
	– ah laytto?
– in hospital _____	– all'ospedale?
	– ahllospaydahlay?
Do I have to go on _____ a special diet?	Devo seguire una dieta?
	Dayvo saygweeray oonah deeaytah?
Am I allowed to travel? _	Mi è permesso viaggiare?
	Mee ay payrmaysso veeahdjahray?
Can I make another _____ appointment?	Potrei fissare un nuovo appuntamento?
	Potrayee feessahray oon nwovo ahppoontahmaynto?
When do I have to _____ come back?	Quando devo ritornare?
	Kwahndo dayvo reetornahray?
I'll come back _____ tomorrow	Ritorno domani
	Reetorno domahny
How do I take this _____ medicine?	Come devo prendere questa medicina?
	Comay dayvo prayndayray kwaystah maydeecheenah?

Deve ritornare domani/fra...giorni

Come back tomorrow/in...days' time.

13.4 Medication and prescriptions

How many capsules/___ drops/injections/ spoonfuls/tablets each time?	Quante capsule/gocce/iniezioni/ cucchiaiate/compresse alla volta? *Kwahntay kahpsoolay/gotchay/ eeneeaytzeeonee/kookkeeaheeahtay/ komprayssay ahllah voltah?*
How many times a ____ day?	Quante volte al giorno? *Kwahntay voltay ahl jorno?*
I've forgotten my _____ medication	Mi sono dimenticato/a le medicine. A casa prendo...
At home I take...	*Mee sono deementeekahto/ah lay maydeecheenay. A kahza prayndo...*
Could you make out a___ prescription for me, please?	Mi potrebbe scrivere una ricetta? *Mee potraybbay skreevayray oonah reechayttah?*

Le prescrivo degli antibiotici/uno sciroppo/un tranquillante/degli analgesici	I'm prescribing antibiotics/a mixture/a tranquilizer/pain killers
Bisogna che si riposi	Have lots of rest
Non può uscire	Stay indoors
Non può alzarsi	Stay in bed

capsule	far sciogliere in	prima di ogni pasto
capsules	acqua	before meals
compresse	dissolve in	queste medicine
tablets	water	influiscono
condurre a termine	gocce	sull'abilità di guida
la cura	drops	this medication
finish the course	inghiottire	impairs your driving
cucchiaio/	swallow (whole)	solo per uso esterno
cucchiaino	ogni...ore	external use only
spoonful/teaspoonful	every...hours	spalmare
iniezioni	pomata	rub on
injections	ointment	...volte al giorno
per...giorni	prendere	...times a day
for...days	take	

13.5 At the dentist's

Do you know a good ___ dentist?	Conosce un buon dentista?
	Konoshay oon bwon daynteestah?
Could you make a _____ dentist's appointment for me? It's urgent	Mi potrebbe prendere un appuntamento urgente dal dentista?
	Mee potraybbay prayndayray oon ahppoontahmaynto oorjenahtay dahl daynteestah?
Can I come in today, ___ please	Posso venire oggi, per favore?
	Posso vayneeray odjee payr fahvoray?
I have a (terrible)_____ toothache	Ho (un) mal di denti (terribile)
	O (oon) mahl dee dayntee (tayrreebeelay)
Could you prescribe/___ give me a painkiller?	Mi potrebbe prescrivere/dare un analgesico?
	Mee potraybbay prayskreevayray/dahray oon ahnahljeezeeko?
I've got a broken tooth _	Ho un dente spezzato
	O oon dayntay spaytzahto

My filling's come out ___	Ho perso un'otturazione
	O payrso oonottoorahtzeeonay
I've got a broken _____ crown	Si è rotta la capsula
	See ay rottah lah kahpsoolah
I'd like/I don't want a___ local anaesthetic	Vorrei essere curato/a con/senza anestesia locale
	Vorrayee ayssayhray koorahto/ah kon/ saynzah ahnaystayzeeah lokahlay
Could you do a _____ temporary repair?	Mi potrebbe curare adesso in modo provvisorio?
	Mee potraybbay koorahray ahdaysso een modo provveezoreeo?
I don't want this tooth ___ pulled	Non voglio un'estrazione
	Non vollyo oonaystrahtzeeonay
My denture is broken. ___ Can you fix it?	Ho rotto la dentiera. La può aggiustare?
	O rotto lah daynteeayhrah. Lah pwo ahdjoostahray?

Qual è il dente che Le fa male?	Which tooth hurts?
Ha un ascesso	You've got an abscess.
Le devo fare una cura canalare	I'll have to do a root canal
Le faccio un'anestesia locale	I'm giving you a local anaesthetic
Devo estrarre/fare un'otturazione/limare questo dente	I'll have to pull/fill/file this tooth
Devo trapanarlo	I'll have to drill it
Apra la bocca	Open wide, please
Chiuda la bocca	Close your mouth, please
Si sciacqui la bocca	Rinse, please
Sente ancora dolore?	Does it hurt still?

14.1 Asking for help

Help! _____	Aiuto!
	Ayooto!
Fire! _____	Al fuoco!
	Ahl fwoko!
Police! _____	Polizia!
	Poleetzeeah!
Quick/Hurry! _____	Presto!
	Praysto!
Danger! _____	Pericolo!
	Payreekolo!
Watch out! _____	Attenzione!
	Attayntzeeonay!
Stop! _____	Alt!/Stop!
	Ahlt!/Stop!
Be careful!/Go easy! ___	Attenzione!/Piano!
	Attayntzeeonay!/Peeahno!
Get your hands off me! _	Giù le mani!
	Joo lay mahnee!
Let go! _____	Lascia!
	Lahshah!
Stop thief! _____	Al ladro!
	Ahl lahdro!
Could you help me, ____ please?	Mi potrebbe aiutare?
	Mee potraybbay aheeootahray?
Where's the police _____ station/emergency exit/fire escape?	Dov'è la questura/l'uscita di emergenza/la scala di sicurezza?
	Dovay ay lah kwaystoorah/loosheetah dee aymayrjayntzah/lah skahlah dee seekooraytzah?
Where's the nearest ____ fire extinguisher?	Dov'è un estintore?
	Dovay ay oonaysteentoray?
Call the fire brigade! ___	Chiami i pompieri!
	Keeahmee ee pompeeayhree!

Call the police! _____	Chiami la polizia!
	Keeahmee lah poleetzeeah!
Call an ambulance! ____	Chiami un'ambulanza!
	Keeahmee oonahmboolahntzah!
Where's the nearest____ phone?	Dov'è un telefono?
	Dovay ay oon taylayfono?
Could I use your _____ phone?	Potrei servirmi del Suo telefono?
	Potrayee sayrveermee dayl soo-o taylayfono?
What's the emergency _ number?	Qual è il numero dei servizi di emergenza?
	Kwahlay ay eel noomayro dayee sayrveetzee dee aymayrjayntzah?
What's the number for _ the police?	Qual è il numero della polizia?
	Kwahlay ay eel noomayro dayllah poleetzeeah?

14.2 Loss

I've lost my wallet/ ____ purse	Ho perso il portafoglio/portamonete
	O payrso eel portahfollyo/portahmonaytay
I lost my...here _____ yesterday	Ieri ho dimenticato qui...
	Eeayree oh deemayteekahto kwee...
I left my...here _____	Ho lasciato qui il mio.../la mia...
	O lahsheeahto kwee eel meeo.../lah meeah...
Did you find my...? ____	Ha trovato il mio /la mia...?
	Ah trovahto eel meeo /lah meeah...?
It was right here _____	Stava qui
	Stahvah kwee
It's very valuable _____	E' molto prezioso/a
	Ay molto praytzeeozo/ah
Where's the lost _____ property office?	Dov'è l'ufficio oggetti smarriti?
	Dovay ay looffeetcheeo odjayttee smahrreetee?

14.3 Accidents

There's been an _____ accident	C'è stato un incidente
	Chay stahto ooneencheedayntay
Someone's fallen into __ the water	Qualcuno è caduto nell'acqua
	Kwahlkoono ay kahdooto nayllahkwah
There's a fire _____	C'è un incendio
	Chay ooneenchayndyo
Is anyone hurt?_____	Ci sono dei feriti?
	Chee sono dayee fayhreetee?
(Nobody) someone has_ been injured	(Non) ci sono dei feriti
	(Non) chee sono day fayhreetee
Someone's still _____ trapped inside the car/train	C'è ancora qualcuno intrappolato dentro la macchina/il treno
	Chay ahnkorah kwahlkoono eentrahppolahto dayntro lah mahkkeenah/eel trayno
It's not too bad. Don't __ worry	Non è grave. Non si preoccupi
	Non ay grahvay. Non see prayokkoopee
Leave everything the ___ way it is, please	Lasci tutto così com'è, per piacere
	Lahshee tootto kozee komay ay, payr peeahchayray
I want to talk to the ____ police first	Vorrei parlare prima alla polizia
	Vorrayee pahrlahray preemah ahllah poleetzeeah
I want to take a_____ photo first	Vorrei prima fare una foto
	Vorrayee preemah fahray oonah foto
Here's my name _____ and address	Ecco il mio nome e il mio indirizzo
	Ekko eel meeo nomay ay eel meeo eendeereeetzo
May I have your name__ and address?	Potrei sapere il Suo nome e il Suo indirizzo?
	Potrayee sahpayray eel soo-o nomay ay ee soo-o eendeereeetzo?

Could I see your _____ identity card/your insurance papers?	Potrei vedere la Sua carta d'identità/i documenti dell'assicurazione?
	Potrayee vaydayray lah sooah kahrtah deedaynteetah/ee dokoomentee dayllasseekoorahtzeeonay?
Will you act as a_____ witness?	Accetta di testimoniare?
	Ahtchayttah dee taysteemoneeahray?
I need this information _ for insurance purposes	Ho bisogno di questi dati per via dell'assicurazione
	O beezoneeo dee kwaystee dahtee payr veeah dayllahsseekoorahtzeeonay
Are you insured? _____	E' assicurato/a?
	Ay ahsseekoorahto/ah?
Third party or _____ comprehensive?	Responsabilità civile o assicurazione completa?
	Raysponsahbeeleetah cheeveelay o ahsseekoorahtzeeonay komplaytah?
Could you sign here, ___ please?	Firmi qui, per favore
	Feermee kwee, payr fahvoray

14.4 Theft

I've been robbed _____	Sono stato/a derubato/a
	Sono stahto/ah dayroobahto/ah
My...has been stolen ___	Hanno rubato il mio.../la mia...
	Ahnno roobahto eel meeo.../lah meeah...
My car's been _____ broken into	Mi hanno forzato la macchina
	Mee ahnno fortzahto la mahkkeenah

14.5 Missing person

I've lost my child/_____ grandmother	Ho perso mio figlio/mia figlia/mia nonna
	O payrso meeo feellyo/meeah feellyah/ meeah nonnah
Could you help me _____ find him/her?	Mi potrebbe aiutare a cercarlo/cercarla?
	Mee potraybbay aheeootahray ah chayrkahrlo/chayrkahrlah?
Have you seen a _____ small child?	Ha visto un bambino/una bambina?
	Ah veesto oon bahmbeeno/oonah bahmbeenah?
He's/she's...years old __	Ha...anni
	Ah...annee
He/she's got...hair _____	Ha i capelli...
	Ah ee kahpayllee...
short/long/blond/red/ __ brown/black/grey/ curly/straight/ frizzy	corti/lunghi/biondi/rossi/bruni/neri/grigi/ ricci/lisci/crespi
	kortee/loongee/beeondee/rossee/broonee/ nayree/ greejee/reetchee/krayspee
– a ponytail _____	– con la coda di cavallo
	– kon lah kodah dee kahvahllo
– plaits _____	– con le trecce
	– kon llay traytchay
– a bun_____	– con una crocchia
	– kon loonah krokkeeah
He's/she's got_____ blue/brown/green eyes	Ha gli occhi azzurri/bruni/verdi
	Ah lly okkee ahdzoorree/broonee/vayrdee
He/she's wearing _____ swimming trunks/hiking boots	Porta un costume da bagno/gli scarponi
	Portah oon kostoomay dah bahneeo/lly skahrponee
with/without glasses,___ carrying/not carrying a bag	con/senza occhiali, (non) porta una borsa
	kon/saynzah okkeeahlee, (non) portah oonah borsah
He/She is tall/short ____	È alto/a, basso/a
	Ay ahlto/ah, bahsso/ah

This is a photo of _____   Ecco una sua foto
  him/her   *Ekko oonah sooah foto*
He/she must be lost ___   Deve essersi perso/a
                        Dayvay ayssayrsee payrso/ah

14.6 The police

An arrest

Documenti prego	Your (vehicle) documents, please
Ha superato il limite di velocità	You were speeding
E' vietato parcheggiare qui	You're not allowed to park here
Non ha messo soldi nel parcometro/parchimetro	You haven't put money in the 'Pay and display'/parking meter
I fari della sua macchina non funzionano	Your lights aren't working
Le devo fare una multa di....	That's a .....fine
Paga direttamente?	Do you want to pay on the spot?
Deve pagare subito	You'll have to pay on the spot

I don't speak Italian _____   Non parlo l'italiano
                        Non pahrlo leetahleeahno
I didn't see the sign _____   Non ho visto quel cartello
                        Non o veesto kwayl kahrtayllo
I don't understand _____   Non capisco cosa c'è scritto
  what it says   *Non kahpeesko kosah chay skreetto*
I was only doing... _____   Andavo soltanto a...chilometri all'ora
  kilometres an hour   *Ahndahvo soltahnto ah...keelomaytree ahllorah*
I'll have my car _____   Farò controllare la macchina
  checked   *Fahro kontrollahray lah mahkkeenah*

| I was blinded by_____ oncoming lights | Sono stato/a abbagliato/a
Sono stahto/ah ahbbahllyahto/ah |

Dov'è successo?	Where did it happen?
Cosa ha perso?	What's missing?
Cosa hanno rubato?	What's been taken?
Potrei avere la Sua carta d'identità?	Could I see your identity card/some identification?
A che ora è successo?	What time did it happen?
Ci sono dei testimoni?	Are there any witnesses?
Firmi qui, per favore	Sign here, please
Desidera un interprete?	Do you want an interpreter?

At the police station

| I want to report a _____ collision/missing person/rape | Vorrei denunciare uno scontro/uno smarrimento/uno stupro
Vorrayee daynooncheeahray oono skontro/ oono zmahrreemaynto/oono stoopro |
| Could you make a ____ statement, please? | Può fare una dichiarazione scritta, per favore?
Pwo fahray oonah deekeeahrahtzeeonay skreettah, payr fahvoray? |
| Could I have a copy ___ for the insurance? | Mi dia una copia per l'assicurazione
Mee deeah oonah kopeeah payr lahsseekoorahtzeeonay |
| I've lost everything_____ | Ho perso tutto
O payrso tootto |
| I've no money left, I'm__ desperate | Non ho più soldi, sono disperato/a
Non o peeoo soldee, sono deespayrahto/ah |
| Could you lend me a___ little money? | Mi potrebbe prestare qualcosa?
Mee potraybbay praystahray kwahlkosah? |

I'd like an interpreter ___	Vorrei un interprete *Vorrayee ooneentayrprayhtay*
I'm innocent _____	Sono innocente *Sono eennochayntay*
I don't know anything __ about it	Non ne so niente *Non nay so neeayntay*
I want to speak to _____ someone from the British/American/ Australian embassy	Vorrei parlare con qualcuno dell'ambasciata Britannica/Americana/ Australiana *Vorrayee pahrlahray con kwahlkoono dayllahmbahshahtah Breetahnneekah/ Ahmayreekahnah/Ahoostrahleeahnah*
I want a lawyer who____ speaks...	Vorrei un avvocato che parli... *Vorrayee oonahvvokahto kay pahrlee...*

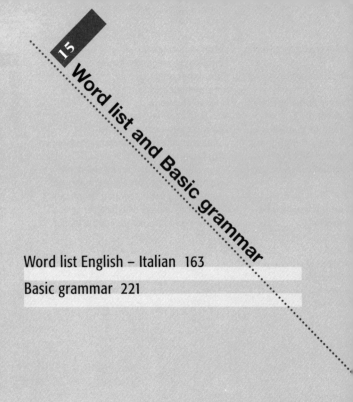

15

Word list and Basic grammar

Word list English – Italian

● **The following word list** is meant to supplement the chapters in this book. Verbs are indicated by the word "verb" and where the gender of a noun is not clear, the word is followed by (m) or (f).

Some of the words not contained in this list can be found elsewhere in the book, eg. in the lists of the car, bicycle and camping equipment. Many food items can be found in the Italian-English list in chapter 4.7

A

about	circa	*cheerkah*
above, up	sopra	*soprah*
abroad	all'estero	*ahllaystayro*
accident	incidente (m)	*eencheedayntay*
adder	vipera	*veepayrah*
address	indirizzo	*eendeereetzo*
admission	ingresso	*eengraysso*
admission price	prezzo del biglietto	*praytzo dayl beellyaytto*
advice	consiglio	*konseellyo*
after	dopo	*dopo*
afternoon	pomeriggio	*pomayreedjo*
aftershave	il dopobarba	*eel dopobahrbah*
again	di nuovo	*dee nwovo*
against	contro	*kontro*
age	età	*aytah*
Aids	Aids (m)	*ayeeds*
air conditioning	aria condizionata	*ahreeah kondeetzeeonahtah*
air sickness bag	busta per vomitare	*boostah payr vomeetahray*
aircraft	aeroplano	*ahayroplahno*
airport	aeroporto	*ahayroporto*
alarm	allarme (m)	*ahllahrmay*
alarm clock	sveglia	*svayllyah*
alcohol	le bevande alcoliche	*lay bayvahnday ahlkoleekay*
all the time	di continuo	*dee konteenoo-o*

allergic	allergico	*ahllayrjeeko*
alone	solo	*solo*
always	sempre	*saympray*
ambulance	ambulanza	*ahmboolahntzah*
amount	somma	*sommah*
amusement park	il 'luna' park	*eel 'loonah' pahrk*
anaesthetize (verb)	anestetizzare	*ahnaystayteetzahray*
anchovy	acciuga	*ahtchoogah*
angry	arrabbiato	*ahrrahbbeeahto*
animal	animale (m)	*ahneemahlay*
ankle	caviglia	*kahveellyah*
answer	risposta	*reespostah*
ant	formica	*formeekah*
anti-diarrhhoea tablets	medicina astringente	*maydeecheenah ahstreenjayntay*
antibiotics	gli antibiotici	*lly ahnteebeeoteechee*
antifreeze	antigelo	*ahnteejaylo*
antique	antico	*ahnteeko*
antiques	gli oggetti antichi	*lly odjayttee ahnteekee*
anus	ano	*ahno*
apartment	appartamento	*ahppahrtahmaynto*
aperitif	aperitivo	*ahpayreeteevo*
apple	mela	*maylah*
apple juice	succo di mela	*sookko dee maylah*
apple pie	torta di mele	*tortah dee maylay*
apple sauce	passato di mele	*pahssahto dee maylay*
appointment	appuntamento	*ahppoontahmaynto*
apricot	albicocca	*ahlbeekokkah*
April	aprile (m)	*ahpreellay*
architecture	architettura	*ahrkeetayttoorah*
area	i dintorni	*ee deentornee*
arm	braccio	*brahtcheeo*
arrive (verb)	arrivare	*ahrreevahray*
arrow	freccia	*fraytchah*
art	arte (f)	*ahrtay*
artery	arteria	*ahrtayreeah*
artichokes	i carciofi	*ee kahrchofee*

article	articolo	*ahrteekolo*
artificial respiration	la respirazione artificiale	*lah rayspeerahtzeeonay ahrteefeechahlay*
arts and crafts	artigianato	*ahrteejahnahto*
ashtray	il portacenere	*eel portahchaynayray*
ask (verb)	chiedere	*keeaydayray*
asparagus	gli asparagi	*lly ahspahrahjee*
aspirin	aspirina	*ahspeereenah*
assault	la violazione	*lah veeolahtzeeonay*
at home	a casa	*ah kahsah*
at night	la/di notte	*lah/dee nottay*
at the back	in fondo	*een fondo*
at the end/at the rear	in fondo	*een fondo*
at the front (theatre etc)	nelle prime file	*nayllay preemay feellay*
at the front	di fronte	*dee frontay*
at the latest	al massimo/al più tardi	*ahl mahsseemo/ ahl peeoo tahrdee*
aubergine	melanzana	*maylahntzahnah*
August	agosto	*ahgosto*
automatic (car)	macchina con il cambio automatico	*mahkkeenah kon eel kahmbeeo ahootomahteeko*
automatic	automatico	*ahootomahteeko*
automatic shutter release	autoscatto	*ahootoskahtto*
autumn	autunno	*ahootoonno*
avalanche	valanga	*vahlahngah*
awake	sveglio	*svayllyo*
awning	tenda da sole	*tayndah dah solay*

B

baby	bambino/a	*bahmbeeno/ah*
baby food (jars of)	gli omogeneizzati	*lly omojaynayeedzahtee*
babysitter	la/il baby-sitter	*lah/eel baybeeseettayr*
back	schiena	*skeeaynah*
bacon	pancetta	*pahnchayttah*

bad	cattivo/male	*kahtteevo/mahlay*
bad/serious	grave	*grahvay*
bag	borsa	*borsah*
baker	panetteria	*pahnayttayreeah*
balcony (theatre)	galleria	*gahllayreeah*
balcony (to building)	il balcone	*eel bahlkonay*
ball	il pallone	*eel pahllonay*
ballet	balletto	*bahllaytto*
ballpoint pen	la biro	*lah beero*
banana	banana	*bahnahnah*
bandage	fascia	*fahsheeah*
bank (river)	riva	*reevah*
bank	banca	*bahnkah*
bar (café)	il bar	*eel bahr*
bar (drinks cabinet)	il bar	*eel bahr*
barbecue	il barbecue	*eel bahrbaykeeoo*
basketball (to play)	giocare a	*jokahray ah*
	pallacanestro	*pahllahkahnaystro*
bath	bagno	*bahneeo*
bath towel	asciugamano da	*ahshoogahmahno*
	bagno	*dah bahneeo*
bathing cap	cuffia da bagno	*cooffeeah dah bahneeo*
bathing cubicle	cabina	*kahbeenah*
bathing suit	il costume da bagno	*eel kostoomay dah*
		bahneeo
bathroom	bagno	*bahneeo*
battery (car)	batteria	*bahttayreeah*
battery	pila	*peellah*
beach	spiaggia	*speeahdjah*
beans	i fagioli	*ee fahjolee*
beautiful	bello	*bayllo*
beauty parlour	istituto di bellezza	*eesteetooto dee bayllaytzah*
bed	letto	*laytto*
bee	ape (f)	*ahpay*
beef	manzo	*mahnzo*
beer	birra	*beerrah*
beetroot	barbabietola	*bahrbahbeeaytolah*

begin (verb)	cominciare	*komeencheeahray*
beginner	il/la principiante	*eel/lah preencheepeeahntay*
behind	dietro	*deeaytro*
belt	cintura	*cheentoorah*
berth	cuccetta	*kootchayttah*
better	meglio	*mayllyo*
bicarbonate of soda	bicarbonato	*beekahrbonahto*
bicycle	bicicletta	*beecheeklayttah*
bicycle pump	pompa della bicicletta	*pompah dayllah beecheeklayttah*
bicycle/motorcycle repairs	riparazioni motociclette e biciclette	*reepahrahtzeeeonee motocheeklayttay ay beecheeklayttay*
bikini	il bikini	*eel beekeenee*
bill	conto	*konto*
billiards, to play	giocare a biliardo	*jokahray ah beellyahrdo*
birthday	compleanno	*komplayahnno*
biscuit	biscotto	*beeskotto*
bite (verb)	mordere	*mordayray*
bitter	amaro	*ahmahro*
black	nero	*nayro*
bland	insipido	*eenseepeedo*
blanket	coperta	*kopayrtah*
bleach (verb)	ossigenare	*osseejaynahray*
blister	vescica	*vaysheekah*
blond	biondo	*beeondo*
blood	il sangue	*eel sahngway*
blood pressure	la pressione (del sangue)	*lah praysseeonay (dayl sahngway)*
blouse	camicetta	*kahmeechayttah*
blow dry (verb)	asciugare con il fon	*ahshoogahray kon eel fon*
blue	azzurro	*ahdzoorro*
boat	barca	*bahrkah*
body	corpo	*korpo*
body milk	il latte per il corpo	*eel lahttay payr eel korpo*
bone	osso	*osso*
bonnet	cofano	*kofahno*

book	libro	*leebro*
book (verb)	prenotare	*praynotahray*
booked	prenotato	*praynotahto*
booking office	ufficio prenotazioni	*ooffeecheeo praynotahtzeeonee*
bookshop	libreria	*leebrayreeah*
boot (car)	il baule	*eel bahoolay*
border	frontiera	*fronteeayrah*
bored (be)	annoiarsi	*ahnnoeeahrsee*
boring	noioso	*noeeozo*
born	nato	*nahto*
borrow	prendere in prestito	*prayndayray een praysteeto*
botanical garden	orto botanico	*orto botahneeko*
both	tutti e due	*toottee ay dooay*
bottle-warmer	lo scaldabiberon	*lo skahldah beebayron*
bottle (baby)	il biberon	*eel beebayron*
bottle	bottiglia	*botteellyah*
box (theatre)	palco	*pahlko*
box	scatola	*skahtolah*
boy	ragazzo	*rahgahtzo*
bra	reggiseno	*raydjeesayno*
bracelet	braccialetto	*brahtchahlaytto*
braised	stufato	*stoofahto*
brake	freno	*frayno*
brake fluid	liquido dei freni	*leekweedo dayee fraynee*
brake oil	olio dei freni	*oleeo dayee fraynee*
brass	ottone (m)	*ottonay*
bread	il pane	*eel pahnay*
break (one's...)	rompersi (la...)	*rompayrsee (lah...)*
breakdown recovery	soccorso stradale	*sokkorso strahdahlay*
breakfast	la (prima) colazione	*lah (preemah) kolahtzeeonay*
breast	petto	*paytto*
bridge	il ponte	*eel pontay*
bring (verb)	portare	*portahray*
brochure	opuscolo	*opooskolo*

broken	rotto	*rotto*
brother	fratello	*frahtayllo*
brown	marrone	*mahrronay*
bruise	livido	*leeveedo*
brush	spazzola	*spahtzolah*
Brussels sprouts	i cavoletti di Bruxelles	*ee kahvolayttee dee Brooxayls*
bubble bath	il bagno schiuma	*eel bahneeo skeeooomah*
bucket	secchio	*saykkeeo*
bug	insetto	*eensaytto*
building	edificio	*aydeefeecho*
buoy	boa	*boah*
burglary	furto (con scasso)	*foorto (kon skahsso)*
burn	bruciatura	*broochahtoorah*
burn (verb)	bruciare	*broochahray*
burnt	bruciato	*broochahto*
bus	autobus (m)	*ahootoboos*
bus station	la stazione degli autobus	*lah stahtzeeonay daylly ahootoboos*
bus stop	fermata dell'autobus	*fayrmahtah dayll-ahootoboos*
business trip	viaggio d'affari	*veeahdjo dahffahree*
busy	occupato	*okkoopahto*
butane camping gas	bombola a gas butano	*bombolah ah gahs bootahno*
butcher	macellaio	*mahchayllaheeo*
butter	burro	*boorro*
buttered roll	panino (con burro)	*pahneeno (kon boorro)*
button	il bottone	*eel bottonay*
buy (verb)	comprare	*komprahray*
by airmail	via aerea	*veeah ahayrayah*

C

cabbage	cavolo	*kahvolo*
cabin	capanna	*kahpahnnah*
cake	torta	*tortah*

cake (small)	pasticcino	pahsteetcheeno
cake shop	pasticcieria	pahsteetcheeayreeah
call (verb)	telefonare/chiamare	taylayfonahraykeeahmahray
call (verb)	chiamare	keeahmahray
called, to be	chiamarsi	keeahmahrsee
camera	macchina fotografica	mahkkeenah fotograhfeekah
camp (verb)	campeggiare	kahmpedjahray
camp shop	il mini-market	eel meenee-mahrkayt
camp site	campeggio	kahmpaydjo
camper	il camper	eel kahmper
camping guide	guida dei campeggi	gweedah dayee kahmpedjee
camping permit	permesso di campeggiare	payrmaysso dee kahmpedjahray
canal boat	battello	bahttayllo
cancel (verb)	annullare	ahnnoollahray
candle	candela	kahndaylah
canoe	canoa	kahnoah
canoe (verb)	andare in canoa	ahndahray een kahnoah
car	macchina	mahkkeenah
car documents	i documenti della macchina	ee dokoomayntee dayllah mahkkeenah
car seat	il sedile	eel saydeellay
car trouble	panne	pahnnay
carafe	caraffa	kahrahffah
caravan	la roulotte	lah roolot
cardigan	il cardigan	eel cahrdeegahn
careful	attenzione	ahttayntzeeoonay
carriage (railway)	il vagone	eel vahgonay
carriageway	carreggiata	kahrraydjhahtah
carrot	carota	kahrotah
carton (cigarettes)	stecca (di sigarette)	stekkah (dee seegahrayttay)
cartridge	cassetta	kahssayttah
cash desk	cassa	kahssah
casino	casinò	kahzeeno
cassette	cassetta	kahssayttah

castle	castello	kahstayllo
cat	gatto	gahtto
catalogue	catalogo	kahtahlogo
cathedral	la cattedrale	lah kahttaydrahlay
cauliflower	il cavolfiore	eel kahvolfeeoray
cave	grotta	grottah
CD	il compact (disk)	eel kompahkt (deesk)
celebrate (verb)	far festa	fahr faystah
cellotape	nastro adesivo	nahstro ahdayzeevo
cemetery	cimitero	cheemeetayro
centimetre	centimetro	chaynteemaytro
central heating	riscaldamento	reeskahldahmaynto
	centrale	chayntrahlay
centre	centro	chayntro
chain	catena	kahtaynah
chair	sedia	saydyeeah
chambermaid	cameriera	kahmayreeayrah
chamois (leather)	camoscio	kahmosho
champagne	lo champagne	lo shahmpahn
change	resto	raysto
change (verb)	cambiare	kahmbeeahray
change the baby's nappy (verb)	cambiare il pannolino	kahmbeeahray eel pahnnoleeno
change the oil (verb)	cambiare l'olio	kahmbeeahray loleeo
chapel	cappella	kahppayllah
charter flight	volo charter	volo chahrtayr
chat up (verb)	fare la corte	fahray lah kortay
check (verb)	controllare	kontrollahray
check in (verb)	fare il check in	fahray eel chaykeen
cheers	cin cin	cheen cheen
cheese (tasty, mild)	formaggio (saporito, delicato)	formahdjo (sahporeeto, dayleekahto)
chef	capo	kahpo
cheque	assegno	ahssayneeo
cheque card	carta assegni	kahrtah ahssaynyee
cherries	le ciliege	lay cheelleeayjay
chess (to play)	(giocare a) scacchi	(jokahray ah) skahkkee

chewing gum	il chewing gum	*eel chayweeng goom*
chicken	pollo	*pollo*
chicory	cicoria	*cheekoreeah*
child	bambino	*bahmbeeno*
child's seat (bicycle)	seggiolino	*saydjeeoleeno*
chilled	fresco	*fraysko*
chin	mento	*maynto*
chips	le patate fritte	*lay pahtahtay freettay*
chocolate	cioccolata	*chokkolahtah*
chocolate (a)	cioccolatino	*chokkolahteeno*
choose (verb)	scegliere	*shayllyayray*
chop	braciola	*brahcholah*
christian name	il nome	*eel nomay*
church	chiesa	*keeayzah*
cigar	sigaro	*seegahro*
cigar shop	tabacchi (m)	*tahbahkkee*
cigarette	sigaretta	*seegahrayttah*
cigarette paper	le cartine	*lay kahrteenay*
cine camera	cinepresa	*cheenaypraysah*
circle	cerchio	*chayrkeeo*
circus	circo	*cheerko*
city hall	municipio	*mooneecheepeeo*
city map	pianta	*peeahntah*
classical concert	concerto di musica	*konchayrto dee*
	classica	*moozeekah klahsseekah*
clean	pulito	*pooleeto*
clean (verb)	pulire	*pooleeray*
clear	chiaro	*keeahro*
clearance	svendita	*svayndeetah*
closed	chiuso	*keeoozo*
closed off (road)	chiuso al traffico	*keeoozo ahl trahffeeko*
clothes	i vestiti	*ee vaysteetee*
clothes hanger	ometto	*omaytto*
clothes peg	molletta da bucato	*mollayttah dah bookahto*
clothing	abbigliamento	*ahbbeellyahmaynto*
coach	il pullman	*eel poollmahn*
coat	soprabito/cappotto	*soprahbeeto/kahppotto*

cockroach	lo scarafaggio	*lo skahrahfahdjo*
cocoa	cacao	*kahkaho*
cod	merluzzo	*mayrlootzo*
coffee	il caffè	*eel kahffay*
coffee filter	filtro del caffè	*feelltro dayl kahffay*
cognac	il cognac	*eel koneeahk*
cold (adj)	freddo	*frayddo*
cold	il raffreddore	*eel rahffrayddoray*
cold cuts	gli affettati	*lly ahffettahtee*
colleague	il/la collega	*eel/lah kollaygah*
collision	lo scontro	*lo skontro*
cologne	eau de toilette (f)	*o day twahlayt*
colour	il colore	*eel koloray*
colour pencils	le matite colorate	*lay mahteetay kolorahtay*
colour TV	il televisore a colori	*eel taylayveezoray ah koloree*
colouring book	album (m) da colorare	*ahlboom dah kolorahray*
comb	il pettine	*eel paytteenay*
come	venire	*vayneeray*
come back (verb)	ritornare	*reetornahray*
compartment	lo scompartimento	*lo skompahrteemaynto*
complaint (med)	disturbo	*deestoorbo*
complaint	reclamo	*rayklahmo*
complaints book	libro reclami	*leebro rayklahmy*
completely	del tutto	*dayl tootto*
compliment	complimento	*kompleemaynto*
compulsory	obbligatorio	*obbleegahtoryeeo*
concert	concerto	*konchayrto*
concert hall	sala dei concerti	*sahlah day konchayrtee*
concussion	la commozione cerebrale	*lah kommotzeeonay chayraybrahlay*
condensed milk	il latte condensato	*eel lahttay kondaynsahto*
condom	preservativo	*praysayrvahteevo*
congratulate (verb)	congratulare	*kongrahtoolahray*
connection	collegamento	*kollaygahmaynto*
constipation	stitichezza	*steeteekaytzah*
consulate	consolato	*konsolahto*

consultation	la consultazione	*lah konsooltahtzeeonay*
contact lens	la lente a contatto	*lah layntay ah kontahtto*
contact lens solution	liquido per lenti a contatto	*leekweedo payr layntee ah kontahtto*
contagious	contagioso	*kontahdjozo*
contraceptive	anticoncezionale (m)	*ahnteekonchaytzeenahlay*
cook (verb)	cucinare	*koocheenahray*
cook	cuoco/a	*kwoko/ah*
copper	il rame	*eel rahmay*
copy	copia	*kopeeah*
corkscrew	il cavatappi	*eel kahvahtahppee*
corn flour	fecola di mais	*faykolah dee mahees*
corner	angolo	*ahngolo*
correct	giusto	*joosto*
correspond (verb)	corrispondere	*korreespondayray*
corridor	corridoio	*korreedoeeo*
costume	il costume	*eel kostoomay*
cot	lettino per il bambino	*laytteeno payr eel bahmbeeno*
cotton	il cotone	*eel kotonay*
cotton wool	il cotone idrofilo	*eel kotonay eedrofeello*
cough	la tosse	*lah tossay*
cough mixture	lo sciroppo per la tosse	*lo sheeroppo payr lah tossay*
counter	banco	*bahnko*
country	campagna	*kahmpahneeah*
country code	prefisso	*prayfeesso*
countryside	il paese	*eel pahaysay*
courgette	zucchina	*dzookkeenah*
course	cura	*koorah*
cousin	cugino/a	*koogeeno/ah*
crab	granchio	*grahnkeeo*
cream	panna	*pahnnah*
cream/ointment (med)	pomata	*pomahtah*
credit card	carta di credito	*kahrtah dee kraydeeto*
crisps	le patatine	*lay pahtahteenay*
croissant	il cornetto	*eel kornaytto*

cross-country run	pista da fondo	*peestah dah fondo*
cross-country skiing	fare dello sci di fondo	*fahray dayllo shee dee fondo*
cross-country skis	gli sci da fondo	*lly shee dah fondo*
cross (the road) (verb)	attraversare (la strada)	*ahttrahvayrsahray (lah strahdah)*
crossing (sea)	traversata	*trahvayrsahtah*
cry (verb)	piangere	*peeahnjayray*
cubic metre	metro cubo	*maytro koobo*
cucumber	cetriolo	*chaytreeolo*
cuddly toy	giocattolo di pelouche	*jokahttolo dee payloosh*
cuff links	i gemelli	*ee jemayllee*
culottes	la gonna pantaloni	*lah gonnah pahntahlonee*
cup	tazza	*tahtzah*
curly	riccio	*reetcheeo*
current	la corrente	*lah korrayntay*
cushion	cuscino	*koosheeno*
custard	crema	*kraymah*
customary	in uso	*een oozo*
customs	dogana	*dogahnah*
customs check	controllo doganale	*kontrollo dogahnahlay*
cut (verb)	tagliare	*tahllyahray*
cutlery	le posate	*lay pozahtay*
cycling	ciclismo	*cheekleesmo*

D

dairy produce	i latticini	*ee lahtteecheenee*
damaged	danneggiato	*dahnnaydjahto*
dance (verb)	ballare	*bahllahray*
dandruff	forfora	*forforah*
danger	pericolo	*payreekolo*
dangerous	pericoloso	*payreekoloso*
dark	scuro	*skooro*
daughter	figlia	*feellyah*
dawn	alba	*ahlbah*

day	giorno	*jorno*
day before yesterday	l'altro ieri	*lahltro eeayree*
dead	morto	*morto*
dear/expensive	caro	*kahro*
decaffeinated	decaffeinato	*daykahffayeenahto*
December	dicembre (m)	*deechaymbray*
deck chair	la sdraio	*lah zdraheeo*
declare (verb)	dichiarare	*deekeeahrahray*
deep	profondo	*profondo*
deep sea diving	gli sport subacquei	*lly sport soobahkwayee*
deepfreeze	il surgelatore	*eel soorjaylahtoray*
degrees	i gradi	*ee grahdee*
delay	ritardo	*reetahrdo*
delicious	ottimo	*otteemo*
dentist	il/la dentista	*eel/lah daynteestah*
dentures	dentiera	*daynteeayrah*
deodorant	il deodorante	*eel dayodorahntay*
department	reparto	*raypahrto*
department store	grande magazzino	*grahnday mahgahdzeeno*
departure	partenza	*pahrtaynzah*
departure time	ora di partenza	*orah dee pahrtaynzah*
depilatory cream	crema depilatoria	*kraymah daypeellahtoreeah*
deposit (verb)	deposito	*daypozeeto*
deposit	caparra	*kahpahrrah*
dessert	il dolce	*eel dolchay*
destination	la destinazione	*lah desteenahtzeeonay*
develop	sviluppare	*sveellooppahray*
diabetic	diabetico	*deeahbeteeko*
dial (verb)	fare	*fahray*
diamond	il diamante	*eel deeahmahntay*
diarrhoea	diarrea	*deeahrrayah*
dictionary	dizionario	*deetzeeonahreeo*
diesel	gasolio	*gahzoleeo*
diesel oil	olio per motori diesel	*oleeo payr motoree deesayl*
diet	dieta	*deeaytah*
difficulty	difficoltà	*deeffeekoltah*
dine (verb)	cenare	*chaynahray*

dining room	sala da pranzo	*sahlah dah prahntzo*
dining/buffet car	carrozza ristorante	*kahrrotza/ reestorahntay*
dinner	cena	*chaynah*
dinner jacket	lo smoking	*lo smokeeng*
direction	la direzione	*lah deeraytzeeonay*
directly	direttamente	*deerayttahmayntay*
dirty	sporco	*sporko*
disabled	disabile	*deezahbeellay*
disco	discoteca	*deeskotaykah*
discount	lo sconto	*lo skonto*
dish	piatto	*peeahtto*
dish of the day	piatto del giorno	*peeahtto dayl jorno*
disinfectant	il disinfettante	*ll deeseenfettahntay*
distance	distanza	*deestahntzah*
distilled water	acqua distillata	*ahkwah deesteellahtah*
disturb (verb)	disturbare	*deestoorbahray*
disturbance	disturbo	*deestoorbo*
dive (verb)	tuffarsi	*tooffahrsee*
diving	gli sport subacquei	*lly sport soobahkwayee*
diving board	trampolino	*trahmpoleeno*
diving gear	attrezzatura da sub	*ahttraytzahtoorah dah soob*
divorced	divorziato	*deevortzeeahto*
DIY-shop	negozio fai-da-te	*negotzeeo fahee-dah-tay*
dizzy (be)	avere il capogiro	*ahvayray eel kahpogeero*
do (verb)	fare	*fahray*
doctor	medico	*maydeeko*
dog	il cane	*eel kahnay*
doll	bambola	*bahmbolah*
domestic	domestico	*domaysteeko*
done (cooked)	cotto	*kotto*
door	porta	*portah*
double	doppio	*doppeeo*
down	giù	*joo*
draught	esserci corrente	*ayssayrchee korrayntay*
draughts (play)	giocare a dama	*jokahray ah dahmah*
dream (verb)	sognare	*soneeahray*
dress	vestito	*vaysteeto*

dressing gown	vestaglia	*vaystahllyah*
drink (verb)	bere	*bayray*
drinking chocolate	cacao	*kahkaho*
drinking water	acqua potabile	*ahkwah potahbeellay*
drive (verb)	guidare	*gweedahray*
driver	autista (m/f)	*ahooteestah*
driving licence	la patente (di guida)	*lah pahtayntay (dee gweedah)*
drought	siccità	*seetcheetah*
dry (verb)	asciugare	*ahshoogahray*
dry	secco	*saykko*
dry clean (verb)	lavare a secco	*lahvahray ah sekko*
dry cleaner's	lavanderia a secco	*lahvahndayreeah ah saykko*
dry shampoo	lo shampoo in polvere	*lo shahmpo een polvayray*
dummy	succhiotto	*sookkeeotto*
during	durante	*doorahntay*
during the day	di giorno	*dee jorno*

E

ear	orecchio	*oraykkeeo*
ear, nose and throat (ENT) specialist	otorinolaringoiatra	*otoreenolahreengoeeahtrah*
earache	il mal d'orecchio	*eel mahl dorekkeeo*
eardrops	le gocce per le orecchie	*lay gotchay payr lay oraykkeeay*
early	presto	*praysto*
earrings	gli orecchini	*lly oraykkeenee*
earth	terra	*tayrrah*
earthenware	ceramica	*chayrahmeekah*
east	est	*ayst*
easy	facile	*fahcheellay*
eat (verb)	mangiare	*mahnjahray*
eczema	eczema (m)	*aykzaymah*
eel	anguilla	*ahngweellah*
egg	uovo	*wovo*
elastic band	elastico	*aylahsteeko*

electric	elettrico	*aylayttreeko*
electricity	la corrente	*lah korrayntay*
embassy	ambasciata	*ahmbahshahtah*
emergency brake	freno d'emergenza	*frayno demayrjayntzah*
emergency exit	uscita di sicurezza	*oosheetah dee seekooraytzah*
emergency number	numero d'emergenza	*noomayro daymayrjayntzah*
emergency phone	telefono d'emergenza	*taylayfono dee aymayrjayntzah*
emergency triangle	triangolo d'emergenza	*treeahngolo daymayrjayntzah*
emery board	limetta per le unghie	*leemayttah payr lay oongeeay*
empty	vuoto	*vwoto*
engaged (busy)	occupato	*okkoopahto*
England	Inghilterra	*eengeelltayrrah*
English	inglese	*eenglaysay*
enjoy (verb)	godere	*godayray*
envelope	busta	*boostah*
error	errore (m)	*ayrroray*
escort	accompagnatrice (f)	*ahkkompahneeahtreechay*
evening (in the)	di sera	*dee sayrah*
evening wear	abito da sera	*ahbeeto dah sayrah*
event	avvenimento	*ahvvayneemaynto*
everything	tutto	*tootto*
everywhere	dappertutto	*dahppayrtootto*
examine (verb)	visitare	*veeseetahray*
excavation	gli scavi	*lly skahvee*
excellent	eccellente	*aytchayllayntay*
exchange (verb)	cambiare	*kahmbeeahray*
exchange office	ufficio cambio	*ooffeecho kahmbeeo*
exchange rate	tasso di cambio	*tahsso dee kahmbeeo*
excursion	escursione (f)	*ayskoorseeonay*
excuse me	mi scusi	*mee skoozee*
excuse/pardon me	scusi	*skoozee*
exhibition	mostra	*mostrah*
exit	uscita	*oosheetah*

expenses	le spese	_lay spaysay_
expensive	caro	_kahro_
explain (verb)	spiegare	_speeaygahray_
express	diretto	_deeraytto_
external	esterno	_aystayro_
eye	occhio	_okkeeo_
eye drops	le gocce per gli occhi	_lay gotchay payrlly okkee_
eye shadow	ombretto	_ombraytto_
eye specialist	oculista (m/f)	_okooleestah_
eyeliner	eye-liner (m)	_aheellaheenayr_

F

face	faccia	_fahtchah_
factory	fabbrica	_fahbbreekah_
faith	la fede	_lah fayday_
fall (verb)	cadere	_kahdayray_
family	famiglia	_fahmeellyah_
famous	famoso	_fahmoso_
farm	fattoria	_fahttoreeah_
farmer	agricoltore	_ahgreekoltoray_
fashion	moda	_modah_
fast	presto	_praysto_
father	il padre	_eel pahdray_
fault	colpa	_kolpah_
fax (verb	spedire un fax	_spaydeeray oon fahx_
February	febbraio	_faybbraheeo_
feel (verb)	sentire	_saynteeray_
feel sick (verb)	avere la nausea	_ahvayray lah nahoozayah_
fence	cancello	_kahnchayllo_
ferry	traghetto	_trahgaytto_
fever	la febbre	_lah faybbray_
fill (verb)	otturare (un dente)	_ottoorahray (oon dayntay)_
fill out (verb)	compilare	_kompeellahray_
filling	otturazione (f)	_ottoorahtzeeonay_
film (photographic)	rullino	_roolleeno_
film	il film	_eel feellm_

filter	filtro	*feelltro*
find (verb)	trovare	*trovahray*
fine (delicate)	fine	*feenay*
fine	multa	*mooltah*
finger	dito	*deeto*
fire	fuoco	*fwoko*
fire (accident)	incendio	*eenchayndeeo*
fire brigade	i pompieri/i vigili	*ee pompee-ayree/ee*
	del fuoco	*veejeellee dayl fwoko*
fire escape	scala di sicurezza	*skahlah dee seekooraytzah*
fire extinguisher	estintore (m)	*aysteentoray*
first	primo	*preemo*
first aid	pronto soccorso	*pronto sokkorso*
first class	prima classe	*preemah klahssay*
fish (verb)	pescare	*peskahray*
fish	il pesce	*eel payshay*
fishing rod	canna da pesca	*kahnnah dah payskah*
fitness centre	palestra	*pahlaystrah*
fitness training	il fitness	*eel feetness*
fitting room	camerino	*kahmayreeno*
fix (verb)	aggiustare	*ahdjoostahray*
flag	bandiera	*bahndeeayrah*
flash	il flash	*eel flash*
flash bulb	lampada flash	*lahmpahdah flash*
flash cube	cubo flash	*koobo flahsh*
flat	appartamento	*ahppahrtahmaynto*
flea market	mercato delle pulci	*mayrkahto dayllay poolchee*
flight	volo	*volo*
flight number	numero del volo	*noomayro dayl volo*
flood	inondazione (f)	*eenondahtzeeonay*
floor	piano	*peeahno*
flour	farina	*fahreenah*
flu	influenza	*eenflooayntzah*
fly-over	viadotto	*veeahdotto*
fly (verb)	andare in aereo	*ahndahray een ahayrayo*
fly (insect)	mosca	*moskah*
fog	nebbia	*naybbeeah*

foggy (be)	esserci nebbia	*ayssayrchee naybbeeah*
folkloristic	folcloristico	*folkloreesteeko*
follow (verb)	seguire	*saygweeray*
food	cibo	*cheebo*
food poisoning	intossicazione (f)	*eentosseekahtzeeonay*
	alimentare	*ahleemayntahray*
foodstuffs	gli alimentari	*lly ahleemayntahree*
foot	il piede	*eel peeayday*
for hire	a nolo	*ah nolo*
forbidden	vietato	*veeaytahto*
forehead	la fronte	*lah frontay*
foreign	straniero	*strahnyayro*
forget (verb)	dimenticare	*deemaynteekahray*
fork	forchetta	*forkayttah*
form	modulo	*modoolo*
fort	fortezza	*fortaytzah*
forward (verb)	spedire	*spaydeeray*
fountain	fontana	*fontahnah*
fragrant	aromatizzato	*ahromahteedzahto*
frame (for glasses)	montatura	*montahtoorah*
franc	franco	*frahnco*
free (of charge)	gratis	*grahtees*
free	libero	*leebayro*
free time	tempo libero	*taympo leebayro*
freeze (verb)	gelare	*jaylahray*
French	francese	*frahnchaysay*
French bread	filoncino	*feelloncheeno*
fresh	fresco	*fraysko*
Friday	il venerdì	*eel vaynayrdee*
fried	fritto	*freetto*
friend	amico/a	*ahmeeko/ah*
friendly	gentile	*jaynteellay*
frightened (be)	avere paura	*ahvayray pahoorah*
fringe	frangetta	*frahnjayttah*
fruit	frutta	*froottah*
fruit juice	succo di frutta	*sookko dee froottah*
frying pan	padella	*pahdayllah*

| full | pieno | *peeayno* |
| fun | divertimento | *deevayrteemaynto* |

G

gallery	galleria	*gahllayreeah*
game	gioco	*joko*
garage	il garage	*eel gahrahdj*
garbage bag	sacco per i rifiuti	*sahkko payr ee reefeeootee*
garden	giardino	*jahrdeeno*
gastroenteritis	la gastroenterite	*lah gahstroayntayreetay*
gauze	garza idrofila	*gahrdzah eedrofeellah*
gear	marcia	*mahrchah*
gel	il gel	*eel jayl*
German	tedesco	*taydaysko*
get off	scendere	*shayndayray*
gift	regalo	*raygahlo*
ginger	lo zenzero	*lo dzayndzayro*
girl	ragazza	*rahgahtzah*
girlfriend	amica	*ahmeekah*
giro cheque	assegno postale	*ahssayneeo postahlay*
giro pass	carta assegni	*kahrtah ahssaynee*
glacier	ghiacciaio	*geeahtcheeaaeeo*
glass (tumbler)	il bicchiere	*eel beekkeeayray*
glass (wine)	vetro	*vaytro*
glasses	gli occhiali	*lly okkeeahlee*
glove	guanto	*gwahnto*
glue	colla	*kollah*
gnat	zanzara	*dzahndzahrah*
go	andare	*ahndahray*
go back (verb)	ritornare	*reetornahray*
go for a walk (verb)	fare una passeggiata	*fahray oonah pahssaydjeeahtah*
go out (verb)	uscire	*oosheeray*
goat's cheese	formaggio caprino	*formahdjo kahpreeno*
gold	oro	*oro*
golf (play)	giocare a golf	*jokahray ah golf*

golf course	campo da golf	*kahmpo dah golf*
gone	sparito	*spahreeto*
good afternoon	buongiorno	*bwonjorno*
good evening	buonasera	*bwonahsayrah*
good morning	buongiorno	*bwonjorno*
good night	buonanotte	*bwonahnottay*
goodbye	addio	*ahddeeo*
gram	grammo	*grahmmo*
grandchild	il/la nipote	*eel/lah neepotay*
grandfather	nonno	*nonno*
grandmother	nonna	*nonnah*
grape	uva	*oovah*
grape juice	succo d'uva	*sookko doovah*
grapefruit	pompelmo	*pompaylmo*
grave	tomba	*tombah*
grease	grasso	*grahsso*
green	verde	*vayrday*
green card	carta verde	*kahrtah vayrday*
greet (verb)	salutare	*sahlootahray*
grey	grigio	*greejo*
grill (verb)	grigliare	*greellyahray*
grilled	alla griglia	*ahllah greellyah*
grocer	gli alimentari	*lly ahleemayntahree*
ground	terra	*tayrrah*
group	gruppo	*grooppo*
guest house	la pensione	*lah paynseeonay*
guide (book)	guida	*gweedah*
guide (person)	guida	*gweedah*
guided tour	visita guidata	*veeseetah gweedahtah*
gynaecologist	ginecologo	*jeenaykologo*

H

hair	i capelli	*ee cahpaylly*
hairbrush	spazzola	*spahtzolah*
hairdresser	il parrucchiere	*eel pahrrookkeeayray*
hairpins	le forcine	*lay forcheenay*

hairspray	lacca	*lahkkah*
half	metà	*maytah*
half full	pieno a metà	*peeayno ah maytah*
half/middle	mezzo	*maydzo*
ham (boiled)	prosciutto (cotto)	*proshootto (kotto)*
ham (raw)	prosciutto (crudo)	*proshootto (kroodo)*
hammer	martello	*mahrtayllo*
hand	la mano	*lah mahno*
hand brake	freno a mano	*frayno ah mahno*
hand-glider	deltaplano	*dayltahplahno*
handbag	borsa	*borsah*
handkerchief	fazzoletto	*fahtzolaytto*
handmade	fatto a mano	*fahtto ah mahno*
happy	felice	*fayleechay*
harbour	porto	*porto*
hard	duro	*dooro*
hat	cappello	*kahppayllo*
have a light (verb)	avere da accendere	*ahvayray dah ahtchayndayray*
hayfever	la febbre da fieno	*lah febbray dah feeayno*
hazelnut	nocciola	*notcholah*
head	testa	*taystah*
headache	il mal di testa	*eel mahl dee testah*
health	la salute	*lah sahlootay*
health food shop	erboristeria	*ayrboreestayreeah*
hear (verb)	sentire	*saynteeray*
hearing aid	apparecchio acustico	*ahppahraykkeeo ahkoosteeko*
heart	il cuore	*eel kworay*
heart patient	malato di cuore	*mahlahto dee kworay*
heat	il caldo	*eel kahldo*
heater	riscaldamento	*reeskahldahmaynto*
heavy	pesante	*payzahntay*
heel	calcagno	*kahlkahneeo*
heel (shoe)	tacco	*tahkko*
hello, goodbye	ciao	*chaho*
helmet	casco	*kahsko*

help (verb)	aiutare/dare una mano	aeeootahray/dahray oonah mahno
help	aiuto	aheeooto
helping (of food)	la porzione	lah portzeeonay
herbal tea	infuso	eenfooso
herbs	le erbe aromatiche	lay ayrbay ahromahteekay
here	qui	kwee
herring	aringa	ahreengah
high	alto	ahlto
high tide	alta marea	ahltah mahrayah
highchair	il seggiolone	eel saydjeeolonay
hiking boots	gli scarponi	lly skahrponee
hip	anca	ahnkah
hire	prendere a nolo	prayndayray ah nolo
historic town centre	centro storico	chayntro storeeko
hitchhike (verb)	fare l'autostop	fahray lahootostop
hobby	hobby (m)	obbee
hold-up	colpo di mano	kolpo dee mahno
holiday (public)	giorno festivo	jorno faysteevo
holiday park	villaggio turistico	veellahdjeeo tooreesteeko
holidays	le vacanze	lay vahkahntzay
homesickness	nostalgia	nostahljeeah
honest	onesto	onaysto
honey	il miele	eel meeayllay
horrible	orribile	orreebeellay
horse	cavallo	kahvahllo
hospital	ospedale (m)	ospaydahlay
hospitality	ospitalità	ospeetahleetah
hot-water bottle	borsa dell'acqua calda	borsah dayllahkwah kahldah
hot, warm	caldo	kahldo
hotel	albergo	ahlbayrgo
hour	ora	orah
house	casa	kahsah
household items	i casalinghi	ee kahsahleengee
houses of parliament	palazzo del parlamento	pahlahtzo dayl pahrlahmaynto

housewife	casalinga	*kahsahleengah*
how far?	quanto è lontano?	*kwahnto ay lontahno?*
how long?	quanto tempo?	*kwahnto taympo?*
how much?	quanto?	*kwahnto?*
hundred grams	etto	*aytto*
hungry (be)	avere fame	*ahvayray fahmay*
hurricane	uragano	*oorahgahno*
hurry	fretta	*frayttah*
husband	marito	*mahreeto*
hut	cabina	*kahbeenah*
hyperventilation	iperventilazione (f)	*eepayrvaynteellah tzeeonay*

I

ice (cubes)	ghiaccio	*gheeahtcheeo*
ice skate (verb)	pattinare	*pahtteenahray*
icecream	gelato	*jaylahto*
idea	idea	*eedayah*
identify (verb)	identificare	*eedaynteefeekahray*
identity card	carta d'identità	*kahrtah deedaynteetah*
ignition key	la chiave	*lah keeahvay*
	d'accensione	*dahtchaynseeonay*
ill	malato	*mahlahto*
illness	malattia	*mahlahtteeah*
imagine (verb)	immaginarsi	*eemmahjeennahrsee*
immediately	subito	*soobeeto*
import duty	tassa	*tahssah*
	d'importazione	*deemportahtzeeonay*
impossible	impossibile	*eemposseebeellay*
in	in	*een*
in love with (be)	essere innamorato di	*essayray eennahmorahto dee*
included	incluso	*eenklooso*
indicate (verb)	indicare	*eendeekahray*
indicator	indicatore (m) di	*eendeekahtoray dee*
	direzione	*deeraytzeeonay*
inexpensive	a buon mercato	*ah bwon mayrkahto*

infection (viral, bacterial)	infezione (f) (virale, batterica)	*eenfetzeeonay (veerahlay, bahttayreekah)*
inflammation	infiammazione (f)	*eenfeeahmmahtzeeonay*
information	informazione (f)	*eenformahtzeeonay*
information office	ufficio informazioni	*ooffeecheeo eenformahtzeeonee*
injection	iniezione (f)	*eenyeetzeeonay*
injured	ferito	*fayreeto*
inner ear	orecchio interno	*oraykkeeo eentayrno*
inner tube	camera d'aria	*kahmayrah dahreeah*
innocent	innocente	*eennochayntay*
insect	insetto	*eensaytto*
insect bite	puntura d'insetto	*poontoorah deensaytto*
insect repellant	insettifugo	*eensaytteefoogo*
inside	dentro	*dayntro*
insurance	assicurazione (f)	*ahsseekoorahtzeeonay*
intermission	intervallo	*eentayrvahllo*
international	internazionale	*eentayrnahtzeeonahlay*
interpreter	interprete (m/f)	*eentayrpraytay*
intersection, crossing	incrocio	*eenkrocheeo*
introduce (verb)	presentare	*praysayntahray*
invite (verb)	invitare	*eenveetahray*
iodine	(tintura di) iodio	*(teentoorah dee) eeodeeo*
Ireland	Irlanda	*Eerlahndah*
iron (metal)	ferro	*fayrro*
iron (verb)	stirare	*steerahray*
iron	ferro da stiro	*fayrro dah steero*
ironing board	tavolo da stiro	*tahvolo dah steero*
island	isola	*eezolah*
Italian	italiano	*eetahleeahno*
itch	prurito	*prooreeto*

J

jack	il cric	*eel kreek*
jacket	giacca	*jahkkah*
jam	marmellata	*mahrmayllahtah*

January	gennaio	*jaynnaheeo*
jar	barattolo	*bahrahttolo*
jaw	mascella	*mahshayllah*
jellyfish	medusa	*maydoosah*
jeweller	gioielleria	*joeeayllayreeah*
jewellery	i gioielli	*ee joyayllee*
jog (verb)	fare il footing	*fahray eel footeeng*
joke	lo scherzo	*lo skayrtzo*
juice	succo	*sookko*
July	luglio	*loolyo*
jumble sale	vendita di beneficenza	*vayndeetah dee baynayfeechayntzah*
jump leads	cavetto del caricabatteria	*kahvetto dayl kahreekahbahttayreeah*
jumper	il maglione	*eel mahllyonay*
June	giugno	*jooneeo*

K

key	la chiave	*lah keeahvay*
kilo	chilo	*keello*
kilometre	chilometro	*keellomaytro*
kind	simpatico	*seempahteeko*
kiss (verb)	baciare	*bahcheeahray*
kiss	bacio	*bahcheeo*
kitchen	cucina	*koocheenah*
knee	ginocchio	*jeenokkeeo*
knee socks	i calzettoni	*ee kahltzettonee*
knife	coltello	*koltayllo*
knit	lavorare a maglia	*lahvorahray ah mahleeah*
know (verb)	sapere	*sahpayray*

L

| lace | pizzo | *peetzo* |
| ladies toilet | gabinetto per signore | *gahbeenaytto payr seeneeeoray* |

lake	lago	*lahgo*
lamp	lampada	*lahmpahdah*
land (verb)	atterrare	*ahttayrrahray*
lane	corsia	*korseeah*
language	lingua	*leengwah*
lard	lardo	*lahrdo*
large	grande	*grahnday*
last	ultimo	*oolteemo*
last night	ieri notte	*eeayree nottay*
late	tardi	*tahrdee*
later	più tardi	*peeoo tahrdee*
laugh (verb)	ridere	*reedayray*
launderette	lavanderia	*lahvahndayreeah*
law	diritto	*deereetto*
laxative	lassativo	*lahssahteevo*
leather	la pelle/cuoio	*lah payllay/kwoeeo*
leather goods	pelletteria	*payllayttayreeah*
leave (verb)	partire	*pahrteeray*
leek	porro	*porro*
left (on the)	a sinistra	*ah seeneestrah*
left	sinistra	*seeneestrah*
left luggage	deposito bagagli	*daypozeeto bahgahlly*
leg	gamba	*gahmbah*
lemon	il limone	*eel leemonay*
lend	prestare	*praystahray*
lens	obiettivo	*obeeaytteevo*
lentils	le lenticchie	*lay laynteekkyeeay*
less	meno	*mayno*
lesson	la lezione	*lah laytzeeonay*
letter	lettera	*layttayrah*
lettuce	lattuga	*lahttoogah*
level crossing	passaggio a livello	*pahssahdjeeo ah leevayllo*
library	biblioteca	*beebleeotaykah*
lie (verb)	mentire	*maynteeray*
life guard	bagnino	*bahneeno*
lift (hitchhike)	passaggio	*pahssahdjo*
lift (in building)	ascensore (m)	*ahshaynsoray*

lift (ski)	seggiovia	*saydjeeoveeah*
light (not dark)	chiaro	*keeahro*
light (not heavy)	leggero	*ledjayro*
lighter	accendino	*ahtchayndeeno*
lighthouse	faro	*fahro*
lightning	il fulmine	*eel foolmeenay*
like (verb)	piacere	*peeahchayray*
line	linea	*leenayah*
linen	lino	*leeno*
lipstick	rossetto	*rossaytto*
liquorice	liquerizia	*leekwayreetzeeah*
listen (verb)	ascoltare	*ahskoltahray*
literature	letteratura	*layttayrahtoorah*
litre	litro	*leetro*
little	poco	*poko*
live (verb)	abitare	*ahbeetahray*
live together (verb)	vivere insieme	*veevayray eenseeaymay*
lobster	aragosta	*ahrahgostah*
local	locale	*lokahlay*
lock	serratura	*sayrrahtoorah*
long	lungo	*loongo*
look (verb)	guardare	*gwahrdahray*
look for (verb)	cercare	*chayrkahray*
lorry	il camion	*eel kahmeeon*
lose (verb)	perdere	*payrdayray*
loss	perdita	*payrdeetah*
lost (be)	perdersi	*payrdayrsee*
lost	perso	*payrso*
lost item	oggetto smarrito	*odjaytto zmahrreeto*
lost property office	ufficio oggetti smarriti	*ooffeecheeo odjayttee smahrreetee*
lotion	la lozione	*lah lotzeeonay*
loud	forte	*fortay*
love	amore (m)	*ahmoray*
love (verb)	amare	*ahmahray*
low	basso	*bahsso*
low tide	bassa marea	*bahssah mahrayah*

LPG	il gas liquido	*eel gahs leeqweedo*
luck	fortuna	*fortoonah*
luggage	i bagagli	*ee bahgahlly*
luggage locker	armadietto	*ahrmahdeeaytto*
lunch	pranzo	*prahntzo*
lungs	i polmoni	*ee polmonee*

M

macaroni	i maccheroni	*ee mahkkayronee*
madam	signora	*seeneeeorah*
magazine	rivista	*reeveestah*
mail	posta	*postah*
main post office	posta centrale	*postah chayntrahlay*
main road	strada maestra	*strahdah mahaystrah*
make an	fissare un	*feessahray oon*
appointment (verb)	appuntamento	*ahppoontahmaynto*
make love	fare l'amore	*fahray lahmoray*
makeshift	provvisorio	*provveezoreeo*
man	uomo	*womo*
manager	il direttore	*eel deerayttoray*
manicure	manicure	*mahneekooray*
map	pianta/mappa	*peeahntah/mahppah*
marble	marmo	*mahrmo*
March	marzo	*mahrtzo*
margarine	margarina	*mahrgahreenah*
marina	porto turistico	*porto tooreesteeko*
market	mercato	*mayrkahto*
marriage	matrimonio	*mahtreemoneeo*
married	sposato	*sposahto*
marry (verb)	sposarsi	*sposahrsee*
mass	messa	*mayssah*
massage	massaggio	*mahssahdjo*
mat	opaco	*opahko*
match	partita	*pahrteetah*
matches	i fiammiferi	*ee feeahmmeefayree*
May	maggio	*mahdjo*

maybe	forse	forsay
mayonnaise	la maionese	lah maheeonaysay
mayor	sindaco	seendahko
meal	pasto	pahsto
mean (verb)	significare	seeneefeekkahray
meat	la carne	lah kahrnay
medication	farmaco	fahrmahko
medicine	medicina	maydeecheenah
meet (verb)	conoscere	konoshayray
melon	il melone	eel maylonay
member (be a)	essere socio	essayray socho
menstruate (verb)	avere le mestruazioni	ahvayray lay maystrooahtzeeonee
menstruation	la mestruazione	lah maystrooahtzeeonee
menu	il menù	eel maynoo
menu of the day	il menù del giorno	eel maynoo dayl jorno
message	messaggio	mayssahdjo
metal	metallo	maytahllo
meter (in cab)	tassametro	tahssahmaytro
metre	metro	maytro
migraine	emicrania	aymeekrahneeah
mild (tobacco)	leggero	ledjeeayro
milk	il latte	eel lahttay
millimetre	millimetro	meelleemaytro
mince	la carne tritata	lah kahrnay treetahtah
mineral water	acqua minerale	ahkwah meenayrahlay
minute	minuto	meenooto
mirror	lo specchio	lo spekkeeo
miss (verb)	mancare	mahnkahray
missing (be)	essere sparito	essayray spahreeto
missing (be) (verb)	mancare	mahnkahray
mistake	lo sbaglio	lo sbahllyo
mistaken (be)	sbagliarsi	sbahllyahrsee
misunderstanding	malinteso	mahleentayzo
modern art	arte moderna	ahrtay modayrnah
moment	attimo/momento	ahtteemo/momaynto
monastery	monastero	monahstayro

Monday	il lunedì	*eel loonaydee*
money	i soldi	*ee soldee*
month	il mese	*eel maysay*
moped	motorino	*motoreeno*
morning-after pill	pillola del giorno dopo	*peellolah dayl jorno dopo*
morning (in the)	la mattina	*lah mahtteenah*
mosque	moschea	*moskayah*
motel	il motel	*eel motayl*
mother	la madre	*lah mahdray*
motor cross	il motocross	*eel motocross*
motorbike	la moto(cicletta)	*lah moto(cheeklayttah)*
motorboat	motoscafo	*motoskahfo*
motorway	autostrada	*ahootostrahdah*
mountain	montagna	*montahneeah*
mountain hut	rifugio alpino	*reefoojo ahlpeeno*
mountaineering	alpinismo	*ahlpeeneesmo*
mouse	topo	*topo*
mouth	bocca	*bokkah*
much/many	molto/molti	*molto/moltee*
multi-storey car park	parcheggio a pagamento	*pahrkedjeeo ah pahgahmaynto*
muscle	muscolo	*mooskolo*
muscle spasms	i crampi muscolari	*ee krahmpee mooskolahree*
museum	museo	*moozayo*
mushrooms	i funghi	*ee foonghee*
music	musica	*moozeekah*
musical	il musical	*eel moozeekahl*
mussels	le cozze	*lay kotzay*
mustard	la senape	*lah saynahpay*

N

nail (on hand)	unghia	*oongeeah*
nail	chiodo	*keeodo*
nail polish	lo smalto per le unghie	*lo smahlto payr lay oongheeay*

nail scissors	le forbicine per unghie	*lay forbeecheenay payr oongheeay*
naked	nudo	*noodo*
nappy	pannolino	*pahnnoleeno*
National Health Service	servizio sanitario	*sayrveetzeeo sahneetahreeo*
nationality	nazionalità	*nahtzeeonahleetah*
natural	naturale	*nahtoorahlay*
nature	natura	*nahtoorah*
naturism	naturismo	*nahtooreezmo*
near	presso	*praysso*
nearby	vicino	*veecheeno*
necessary	necessario	*nechayssahreeo*
neck	collo	*kollo*
nectarine	la pescanoce	*lah peskahnochay*
needle	ago	*ahgo*
negative	negativa	*naygahteevah*
neighbours	i vicini	*ee veecheenee*
nephew	il nipote	*eel neepotay*
never	mai	*mahee*
new	nuovo	*nwovo*
news	le notizie	*lay noteetzeeay*
news stand	edicola	*aydeekolah*
newspaper	il giornale	*eel jornahlay*
next	prossimo	*prosseemo*
next to	accanto a	*ahkkahnto ah*
nice	piacevole/bello/buono	*peeahchayvolay/bayllo/bwono*
niece	la nipote	*lah neepotay*
night	la notte	*lah nottay*
night duty	servizio notturno	*sayrveetzeeo nottoorno*
night-club	il locale notturno	*eel lokahlay nottoorno*
nightclub	il night	*eel naheet*
nightlife	vita notturna	*veetah nottoornah*
no-one	nessuno	*nessoono*
no	no	*no*
no overtaking	divieto di sorpasso	*deeveeeayto dee sorpahsso*

noise	il rumore	*eel roomoray*
nonsense	le sciocchezze	*lay shokkaytzay*
nonstop	senza scalo	*saynzah skahlo*
normal	normale	*normahlay*
north	nord	*nord*
nose	naso	*nahzo*
nose drops	le gocce per il naso	*lay gotchay payr eel nahzo*
notepaper	carta da lettere	*kahrtah dah layttayray*
nothing	niente	*neeayntay*
November	novembre (m)	*novaymbray*
nowhere	da nessuna parte	*dah nessoonah pahrtay*
nudist beach	spiaggia per nudisti	*speeahdjah payr noodeestee*
number	numero	*noomayro*
number plate	targa	*tahrgah*
nurse	infermiera	*eenfayrmeeayrah*
nutmeg	la noce moscata	*lah nochay moskahtah*
nuts	le noci	*lay nochee*

O

October	ottobre (m)	*ottobray*
odometer	il contachilometri	*eel kontahkeellomaytree*
off-licence	enoteca	*aynotaykah*
off (of food)	andato a male	*ahndahto ah mahlay*
offer (verb)	offrire	*offreeray*
office	ufficio	*ooffeecheeo*
oil (vegetable)	olio di semi	*oleeo dee saymee*
oil	olio	*oleeo*
oil level	livello dell'olio	*leevayllo daylloleeo*
ointment	pomata	*pomahtah*
ointment for burns	pomata contro le ustioni	*pomahtah kontro lay oosteeonee*
okay	d'accordo	*dahkkordo*
old	vecchio	*vaykkeeo*
olive oil	olio d'oliva	*oleeo doleevah*
olives	le olive	*lay oleevay*

omelette	frittata/omelette (f)	*freettahtah/omaylayt*
on	su/sopra	*soo/soprah*
on board	a bordo	*ah bordo*
oncoming car	veicolo che viene in senso contrario	*vayeekolo kay veeaynay een saynso kontrahryeeo*
one-way traffic	senso unico	*saynso ooneeko*
onion	cipolla	*cheepollah*
open	aperto	*ahpayrto*
open (verb)	aprire	*ahpreeray*
open air (in the)	all'aperto	*ahllahpayrto*
opera	opera	*opayrah*
operate (verb)	operare	*opayrahray*
operator (telephone)	il/la centralinista	*eel/lah chayntrahleeneestah*
operetta	operetta	*opayrayttah*
opposite	di fronte a	*dee frontay ah*
optician	ottico	*otteeko*
orange	arancia	*ahrahnchah*
orange (adj)	arancione	*ahrahncheeonay*
orange juice	spremuta d'arancia	*spraymootah dahrahnchah*
order	ordinazione (f)	*ordeenahtzeeonay*
order (verb)	ordinare	*ordeenahray*
other	altro	*ahltro*
other side	lato opposto	*lahto opposto*
outing	gita	*jeetah*
outside	fuori	*foohoree*
overtake (verb)	sorpassare	*sorpahssahray*
oysters	le ostriche	*lay ostreekay*

P

packed lunch	la colazione al sacco	*lah kolahtzeeonay ahl sahkko*
pain	il dolore/il male	*eel doloray/eel mahlay*
painkiller	analgesico	*ahnahljayzeeko*

paint	la vernice	lah vayrneechay
painting (art)	pittura	peettoorah
painting (object)	quadro	kwahdro
palace	palazzo	pahlahtzo
pancake	la crèpe	lah krayp
pants (ladies')	lo slip	lo sleep
pants, briefs	le mutande	lay mootahnday
panty liner	il salvaslip	eel sahlvahsleep
paper	carta	kahrtah
paraffin oil	olio di paraffina	oleeo dee pahrahffeenah
parasol	ombrellone (m)	ombrayllonay
parcel	pacchetto	pahkkaytto
parents	i genitori	ee jayneetoree
park	parco	pahrko
park (verb)	parcheggiare	pahrkaydjeeahray
parking space	parcheggio	pahrkaydjeeo
parsley	prezzemolo	praytzaymolo
part (spare)	pezzo di ricambio	paytzo dee reekahmbeeo
partner	il/la partner	eel/lah pahrtner
party	festa	faystah
passable	transitabile	trahnseetahbeellay
passenger	passeggero	pahssaydjayro
passport	passaporto	pahssahporto
passport photo	la foto tessera	lah foto tessayrah
patient	il/la paziente	eel/lah pahtzeeeentay
pavement	il marciapiede	eel mahrcheeahpeeayday
pay (verb)	pagare	pahgahray
peach	pesca	payskah
peanuts	le noccioline	lay notcheeoleenay
pear	pera	payrah
peas	i piselli	ee peezayllee
pedal	il pedale	eel pedahlay
pedestrian crossing	attraversamento	ahttrahvayrsahmaynto
	pedonale	paydonahlay
pedicure	il/la pedicure	eel/lah paydeekooray
pen	penna	paynnah
pencil	matita	mahteetah

penis	il pene	*eel paynay*
pepper (red, green)	il peperone (rosso, verde)	*eel paypayronay (rosso, vayrday)*
pepper	il pepe	*eel paypay*
performance	lo spettacolo/la rappresentazione	*lo spayttahkolo/lah rahppraysayntahtzeeonay*
perfume	profumo	*profoomo*
perm (verb)	fare la permanente	*fahray lah payrmahnayntay*
perm	la permanente	*lah payrmahnayntay*
permit	licenza	*leechaynzah*
person	persona	*payrsonah*
personal	personale	*payrsonahlay*
petrol	benzina	*bayndzeenah*
petrol station	il distributore di benzina	*eel deestreebootoray dee bayndzeenah*
pets	gli animali domestici	*lly ahneemahlee domaysteechee*
pharmacy	farmacia	*fahrmahcheeah*
phone (verb)	telefonare	*taylayfonahray*
phone (tele-)	telefono	*taylayfono*
phone box	telefono pubblico	*taylayfono poobbleeko*
phone directory	elenco telefonico	*aylaynko taylayfoneeko*
phone number	numero di telefono	*noomayro dee taylayfono*
photocopier	la copiatrice	*lah copeeahtreechay*
photocopy (verb)	fotocopiare	*fotokopeeahray*
photocopy	fotocopia	*fotokopeeah*
photograph	la foto	*lah foto*
photograph (verb)	fotografare	*fotograhfahray*
pick up (verb)	andare/venire a prendere	*ahndahray/vayneeray ah prayndayray*
pickled	sott'aceto	*sottahchayto*
picnic	il picnic	*eel peekneek*
piece of clothing	capo di vestiario	*kahpo dee vaysteeahreeo*
pier	molo	*molo*
pigeon	il piccione	*eel peetcheeonay*
pill (contraceptive)	pillola (anticoncezionale)	*peellolah (ahnteekonchaytzeeonahlay)*

pillow	il guanciale	*eel gwahncheeahlay*
pillowcase	federa	*faydayrah*
pin	lo spillo	*lo speello*
pineapple	ananas (m)	*ahnahnahs*
pink	rosa	*rozah*
pipe	pipa	*peepah*
pipe tobacco	tabacco da pipa	*tahbahkko dah peepah*
pity	peccato	*pekkahto*
place of interest	monumento	*monoomaynto*
plan, map	la piantina	*lah peeahnteenah*
plant	pianta	*peeahntah*
plasters	i cerotti	*ee chayrottee*
plastic	plastica	*plahsteekah*
plastic bag	busta di plastica	*boostah dee plahsteekah*
plate	piatto	*peeahtto*
platform	binario	*beenahreeo*
play (a)	opera teatrale	*opayrah tayhahtrahlay*
play (verb)	giocare	*jokahray*
playground	parco giochi	*pahrko jokee*
playing cards	le carte da gioco	*lay kahrtay dah joko*
pleasant	piacevole	*peeahchayvolay*
please	per favore	*payr fahvoray*
please (verb)	piacere	*peeahchayray*
pleasure	il piacere	*eel peeahchayray*
plum	prugna	*prooneeah*
pocketknife	temperino	*taympayreeno*
point (verb)	indicare	*eendeekahray*
poison	veleno	*vaylayno*
police	polizia	*poleetzeeah*
police station	questura	*kwaystoorah*
policeman	il vigile	*eel veejeellay*
pond	lo stagno	*lo stahneeo*
pony	il pony	*eel ponee*
pop concert	concerto pop	*konchayrto pop*
population	la popolazione	*lah popolahtzeeonay*
pork	la carne di maiale	*lah kahrnay dee maheeahlay*

port	(vino di) porto	*(veeno dee) porto*
porter (hotel)	portinaio	*porteeonaheeo*
porter (railway)	facchino	*fahkkeeno*
post code	il codice postale	*eel kodeechay postahlay*
post office	ufficio postale	*ooffeecheeo postahlay*
postage	affrancatura	*ahffrahnkahtoorah*
postbox	buca delle lettere	*bookah dayllay layttayray*
postcard	cartolina	*kahrtoleenah*
postman	postino	*posteeno*
potato	patata	*pahtahtah*
poultry	il pollame	*eel pollahmay*
powdered milk	il latte in polvere	*eel lahttay een polvayray*
power point	presa elettrica	*prayzah aylayttreekah*
pram	carrozzina	*kahrrotzeenah*
prawns	i gamberetti	*ee gahmbayrayttee*
prefer (verb)	preferire	*prefayreeray*
preference	preferenza	*prefayrayntzah*
pregnant	incinta	*eencheentah*
present (gift)	regalo	*regahlo*
present (in time)	presente	*prayzayntay*
press (verb)	pigiare	*peejahray*
pressure	la pressione	*lah praysseeonay*
price	prezzo	*praytzo*
price list	listino prezzi	*leesteeno praytzee*
print (verb)	stampare	*stahmpahray*
print	copia	*kopeeah*
probably	probabilmente	*probahbeellmayntay*
problem	il problema	*eel problaymah*
profession	la professione	*lah professeeonay*
programme	il programma	*eel programmah*
pronounce (verb)	pronunciare	*pronoonchahray*
propane camping gas	bombola a gas propano	*bombolah ah gahs propahno*
prune	prugna secca	*prooneeah saykkah*
pudding	budino	*boodeeno*
pull a muscle (verb)	avere uno strappo muscolare	*ahvayray oono strahppo mooskolahray*

pull out (a tooth) (verb)	estrarre (un dente)	*estrahrray (oon dayntay)*
pure	puro	*pooro*
purple	viola	*veeolah*
purse	il portamonete/ borsellino	*eel portahmonaytay/ borsaylleeno*
push (verb)	spingere	*speenjayray*
puzzle	il puzzle	*eel poodzlay*
pyjamas	il pigiama	*eel peejahmah*

Q

quarter	quarto	*kwahrto*
quarter of an hour	quarto d'ora	*kwahrto dorah*
queen	regina	*rayjeenah*
question	domanda	*domahndah*
quick	presto	*praysto*
quiet	tranquillo	*trahnkweello*

R

radio	la radio	*lah rahdeeo*
railways	le ferrovie	*lay fayrroveeay*
rain (verb)	piovere	*peeovayray*
rain	pioggia	*peeodjah*
raincoat	impermeabile (m)	*eempayrmayahbeellay*
raisin	uva secca	*oovah saykkah*
rape	lo stupro	*lo stoopro*
rapids	rapida	*rahpeedah*
raspberries	i lamponi	*ee lahmponee*
raw	crudo	*kroodo*
raw vegetables	le verdure crude	*lay vayrdooray krooday*
razor blades	le lamette	*lay lahmayttay*
read	leggere	*ledjayray*
ready	pronto	*pronto*
receipt (till)	lo scontrino	*lo skontreeno*
receipt	ricevuta	*reechayvootah*

recipe	ricetta	*reechayttah*
reclining chair	sedia a sdraio	*saydeeah ah sdraheeo*
recommend (verb)	consigliare	*konseellyahray*
rectangle	rettangolo	*rayttahngolahray*
red	rosso	*rosso*
red wine	vino rosso	*veeno rosso*
reduction	lo sconto	*lo skonto*
refrigerator	frigorifero	*freegoreefayro*
regards	(tanti) saluti	*(tahntee) sahlootee*
region	la regione	*lah rayjonay*
registered	raccomandato	*rahkkomahndahto*
registration (car)	libretto di circolazione	*leebraytto dee cheerkolahtzeeonay*
relatives	i parenti	*ee pahrayntee*
reliable	affidabile	*ahffeedahbeellay*
religion	la religione	*lah rayleejonay*
rent (verb)	affittare	*ahffeettahray*
rent out (verb)	affittare	*ahffeettahray*
repair (verb)	aggiustare	*ahdjoostahray*
repairs	le riparazioni	*lay reepahrahtzeeonee*
repeat (verb)	ripetere	*reepaytayray*
report	il verbale	*eel vayrbahlay*
responsible	responsabile	*raysponsahbeellay*
rest (verb)	riposare	*reepozahray*
restaurant	il ristorante	*eel reestorahntay*
retired	pensionato	*paynseeonahto*
return (ticket)	andata e ritorno (f)	*ahndahtah ay reetorno*
reverse (vehicle) (verb)	fare marcia indietro	*fahray mahrchah eendeeaaytro*
rheumatism	reumatismo	*rayoomahteezmo*
rice	riso	*reezo*
riding (horseback)	andare a cavallo	*ahndahray ah kahvahllo*
riding school	maneggio	*mahnaydjeeo*
right	destra	*daystrah*
right (on the)	a destra	*ah daystrah*
ripe	maturo	*mahtooro*
risk	rischio	*reeskeeo*

river	il fiume	*eel feeoomay*
road	strada	*strahdah*
roasted	arrostito	*ahrrosteeto*
rock	roccia	*rotchah*
roll (bread)	panino	*pahneeno*
rolling tobacco	tabacco per sigarette	*tahbahkko payr seegahrayttay*
roof rack	il portapacchi	*eel portahpahkkee*
room	camera	*kahmayrah*
room number	numero della camera	*noomayro dayllah kahmayrah*
room service	servizio in camera	*sayrveetzeeo een kahmayrah*
rope	corda	*kordah*
rosé	rosato	*rozahto*
roundabout	rotatoria	*rotahtoreeah*
route	itinerario	*eeteenayrahreeo*
rowing boat	barca a remi	*bahrkah ah raymee*
rubber	gomma	*gommah*
rubbish (silly things)	le sciocchezze	*lay shokkaytzay*
rucksack	lo zaino	*lo dzaheeno*
rude	scortese	*skortayzay*
ruins	le rovine	*lay roveenay*
run into (verb)	incontrare	*eenkontrahray*

S

sad	triste	*treestay*
safari	il safari	*eel sahfahree*
safe (adj)	sicuro	*seekooro*
safe	cassetta di sicurezza	*kahssayttah dee seekooraytzah*
safety pin	spilla di sicurezza	*speellah dee seekooraytzah*
sail (verb)	fare della vela	*fahray dayllah vaylah*
sailing boat	barca a vela	*bahrkah ah vaylah*
salad	insalata	*eensahlahtah*
salami	il salame	*eel sahlahmay*

sale	i saldi	*ee sahldee*
salt	il sale	*eel sahlay*
same	lo stesso	*lo staysso*
sandy beach	spiaggia di sabbia	*speeahdjah dee sahbbeeah*
sanitary pads	gli assorbenti	*lly ahssorbayntee*
sardines	le sardine	*lay sahrdeenay*
satisfied	contento	*kontaynto*
Saturday	sabato	*sahbahto*
sauce	sugo	*soogo*
sausage	salsiccia	*sahlseetchah*
savoury	saporito	*sahporeeto*
say (verb)	dire	*deeray*
scarf	sciarpa	*shahrpah*
scenic walk	itinerario turistico	*eeteenayrahreeo tooreesteeko*
school	scuola	*skwolah*
scissors	le forbici	*lay forbeechee*
scooter	scooter	*skootayr*
scorpion	lo scorpione	*lo skorpeeonay*
Scotland	Scozia	*Scotzeeah*
scrambled eggs	le uova strapazzate	*lay wovah strahpahtzahtay*
screw	la vite	*lah veetay*
screwdriver	il cacciavite	*eel kahtchahveetay*
sculpture	scultura	*skooltoorah*
sea	il mare	*eel mahray*
seasick (be)	avere il mal di mare	*ahvayray eel mahldeemahray*
seat	posto (a sedere)	*posto (ah saydayray)*
second-hand	usato	*oozahto*
second	secondo	*saykondo*
secretion (med)	la secrezione	*lah saykraytzeeonay*
sedative	il tranquillante	*eel trahnkweellahntay*
see (verb)	vedere	*vedayray*
semi-skimmed	parzialmente scremato	*pahrtzeeahlmayntay skraymahto*
send (verb)	spedire	*spaydeeray*
sentence	la frase	*lah frahzay*

English	Italian	Pronunciation
September	settembre (m)	*sayttaymbray*
service (church)	la funzione religiosa	*lah foontzeeonay rayleejozah*
service	servizio	*sayrveetzeeo*
serviette	tovagliolo	*tovahllyolo*
set (of hair) (verb)	mettere in piega	*mayttayray een peeaygah*
sewing thread	filo da cucire	*feello dah koocheeray*
shade	ombra	*ombrah*
shallow	poco profondo	*poko profondo*
shampoo	lo shampoo	*lo shahmpo*
shark	lo squalo	*lo skwahlo*
shave (verb)	farsi la barba	*fahrsee lah bahrbah*
shaver	rasoio	*rahzoyeeo*
shaving brush	pennello da barba	*paynnayllo dah bahrbah*
shaving cream	crema da barba	*kraymah dah bahrbah*
shaving soap	il sapone da barba	*eel sahponay dah bahrbah*
sheet	lenzuolo	*laynzwolo*
sherry	Sherry	*Shayrree*
shirt	camicia	*kahmeechah*
shoe	scarpa	*skahrpah*
shoe polish	lucido da scarpe	*loocheedo dah skahrpay*
shoe shop	calzature	*kahltzahtooray*
shoelace	laccio	*lahtcheeo*
shoemaker	calzolaio	*kahltzolaheeo*
shop	negozio	*negotzeeo*
shop (verb)	fare la spesa	*fahray lah spayzah*
shop assistant	commessa/o	*kommayssah/o*
shop window	vetrina	*vaytreenah*
shopping centre	centro commerciale	*chayntro kommayrchahlay*
short	corto/breve	*korto/brayvay*
short circuit	cortocircuito	*kortocheerkweeto*
shoulder	spalla	*spahllah*
show	lo spettacolo	*lo spayttahkolo*
shower	doccia	*dotcheeah*
shutter	otturatore (m)	*ottoorahtoray*
side	lato	*lahto*
sieve	setaccio	*saytahtcho*

sign	cartello	*kahrtayllo*
sign (verb)	firmare	*feermahray*
silence	silenzio	*seellayntzeeo*
silver	argento	*ahrjaynto*
silver-plated	placcato in argento	*plahkkahto een ahrjaynto*
simple	semplice	*saympleechay*
single (ticket)	andata	*ahndahtah*
single (unmarried)	singolo	*seengolo*
single	singolo	*seengolo*
sir	il signore	*eel seeneeoray*
sister	sorella	*sorayllah*
sit (verb)	sedere	*saydayray*
size	misura/ taglia	*meezoorah/ tahllyah*
ski (verb)	sciare	*sheeahray*
ski boots	gli scarponi da sci	*lly skahrponee dah shee*
ski goggles	gli occhiali da sci	*lly okkeeahlee dah shee*
ski instructor	maestro di sci	*mahaystro dee shee*
ski lessons/class	la lezione di sci	*lah laytzeeonay dee shee*
ski lift	lo ski-lift	*lo skee-leeft*
ski pants	i pantaloni da sci	*ee pahntahlony dah shee*
ski pass	lo ski pass	*lo skee pahss*
ski slope	pista da sci	*peestah dah shee*
ski stick	racchetta	*rahkkayttah*
ski suit	completo da sci	*complayto dah shee*
ski wax	sciolina	*sheeoleenah*
skin	la pelle	*lah payllay*
skirt	gonna	*gonnah*
skis	paio di sci	*paheeo dee shee*
sleep (verb)	dormire	*dormeeray*
sleeping car	la carrozza letto	*lah kahrrotzah laytto*
sleeping pills	i sonniferi	*ee sonneefayree*
slide	diapositiva	*deeahpozeeteevah*
slip	la sottoveste	*lah sottovaystay*
slip road	corsia di accelerazione	*korseeah dee ahtchaylayrahtzeeonay*
slow	lento	*laynto*
slow train	il locale	*eel lokahlay*

small	piccolo	peekkolo
small change	moneta	monaytah
smell (verb)	puzzare	pootzahray
smoke	fumo	foomo
smoke (verb)	fumare	foomahray
smoked	affumicato	ahffoomeekahto
smoking	scompartimento	skompahrteemaynto
compartment	per fumatori	payr foomahtoree
snake	la serpe	lah sayrpay
snorkel	il boccaglio	eel bokkahllyo
snow (verb)	nevicare	nayveekahray
snow	la neve	lah nayvay
snow chains	le catene da neve	lay kahtaynay dah nayvay
soap	il sapone	eel sahponay
soap powder	il sapone in polvere	eel sahponay een polvayray
soccer	calcio	kahlcho
soccer match	partita di calcio	pahrteetah dee kahlcho
socket	presa di corrente	prayzah dee korrayntay
socks	i calzini	ee kahltzeenee
soft drink	bibita/ bevanda	beebeetah/bevahdah
sole (fish)	sogliola	sollyolah
sole (shoe)	suola	swolah
solicitor	avvocato	ahvvokahto
someone	qualcuno	kwahlkoono
sometimes	talvolta	tahlvoltah
somewhere	da qualche parte	dah kwahlkay pahrtay
son	figlio	feellyo
soon	presto	praysto
sorbet	sorbetto	sorbaytto
sore	ulcera	oolchayrah
sore throat	il mal di gola	eel mahl dee golah
sorry	scusami/mi scusi	skoozahmee/mee skoozee
sort	tipo	teepo
soup	zuppa	dzooppah
source	la sorgente	lah sorjayntay
south	il sud	eel sood

souvenir	il souvenir	*eel sooovayneer*
spaghetti	gli spaghetti	*lly spahgayttee*
spanner	la chiave fissa/la	*lah keeahvay*
	chiave per bulloni	*feessah/lah keeahvay*
		payr boollonee
spare	di riserva	*dee reesayrvah*
spare parts	i pezzi di ricambio	*ee paytzee dee*
		reekahmbeeo
spare wheell	ruota di scorta	*rwotah dee skortah*
speak (verb)	parlare	*pahrlahray*
special	straordinario	*strahordeenahreeo*
specialist	lo specialista	*lo spaychahleestah*
specialty	specialità	*spaycheeahleetah*
speed limit	il limite di velocità	*eel leemeetay dee*
		vaylocheetah
spell (verb)	dire come si scrive	*deeray komay see skreevay*
spicy	piccante	*peekkahntay*
splinter	scheggia	*skaydjeeah*
spoon, spoonful	cucchiaio	*kookkeeaheeo*
sport (play)	fare dello sport	*fahray dayllo sport*
sport	lo sport	*lo sport*
sports centre	centro sportivo	*chayntro sporteevo*
spot	posto/luogo	*posto/lwogo*
sprain (verb)	slogarsi	*slogahrsee*
spring	primavera	*preemahvayrah*
square	quadrato	*kwahdrahto*
square (town)	piazza	*peeahtzah*
square metre	metro quadro	*maytro kwahdro*
squash (to play)	giocare a squash	*jokahray ah sqoo-osh*
stadium	lo stadio	*lo stahdeeo*
stain	macchia	*mahkkeeah*
stain remover	lo smacchiatore	*lo smahkkeeaahtoray*
stainless steel	acciaio inossidabile	*ahtcheeaheeo*
		eenosseedahbeellay
stairs	scala	*skahlah*
stalls	platea	*plahtayah*
stamp	francobollo	*frahnkobollo*

start (an engine) (verb)	accendersi/mettere in moto	ahtchayndayrsee/ mayttayray een moto
station	la stazione	lah stahtzeeonay
statue	statua	stahtooah
stay (in hotel) (verb)	essere alloggiato	essayray ahllodjeeahto
stay (verb)	rimanere	reemahnayray
stay	soggiorno	sodjorno
steal (verb)	rubare	roobahray
stench	puzzo	pootzo
sting (verb)	pungere	poonjayray
stitch (med) (verb)	suturare	sootoorahray
stitch (verb)	cucire	koocheeray
stock, broth	brodo	brodo
stockings	le calze	lay kahltzay
stomach	lo stomaco/pancia	lo stomahko/pahnchah
stomach ache	il mal di stomaco/ pancia	eel mahl dee stomahko/pahnchah
stomach cramps	i crampi allo stomaco	ee krahmpy ahllo stomahko
stools	le feci	lay faychee
stop (bus/train)	fermata	fayrmahtah
stop (verb)	fermarsi	fayrmahrsee
stopover	lo scalo	lo skahlo
storm	tempesta	taympaystah
straight	liscio	leesheeo
straight ahead	sempre dritto	saympray dreetto
straw	cannuccia	kahnnootchah
strawberries	le fragole	lay frahgolay
street	strada	strahdah
street side	lato della strada	lahto dayllah strahdah
strike	lo sciopero	lo shopayro
strong	forte	fortay
study (verb)	studiare	stoodeeahray
stuffing	ripieno	reepeeayno
subscriber's number	numero dell'abbonato	noomayro dayllahbbonahto
subtitled	con sottotitoli	kon sottoteetolee
succeed (verb)	riuscire	reeoosheeray
sugar	lo zucchero	lo dzookkayro

sugar lump	zolletta di zucchero	*dzolayttah dee dzookkayro*
suit	abito/completo	*ahbeeto/komplayto*
suitcase	valigia	*vahleedjah*
summer	estate (f)	*aystahtay*
summertime	ora legale	*orah laygahlay*
sun	il sole	*eel solay*
sun hat	cappello di paglia	*kahppayllo dee pahllyah*
sunbathe	prendere il sole	*prayndayray eel solay*
Sunday	domenica	*domayneekah*
sunglasses	gli occhiali da sole	*lly okkeeahlee dah solay*
sunset	tramonto	*trahmonto*
sunstroke	insolazione (f)	*eensolahtzeeoonay*
suntan lotion	olio solare	*oleeo solahray*
supermarket	supermercato	*soopayrmayrkahto*
surcharge	supplemento	*soopplaymaynto*
surf (verb)	fare il surf	*fahray eel soorf*
surf board	tavola da surf	*tahvolah dah soorf*
surgery	ambulatorio	*ahmboolahtoreeo*
surname	il cognome	*eel koneeomay*
surprise	sorpresa	*sorprayzah*
swallow (verb)	inghiottire	*eengeeotteeray*
swamp	la palude	*lah pahlooday*
sweat	il sudore	*eel soodoray*
sweet	caramella	*kahrahmayllah*
sweet (adj)	dolce	*dolchay*
sweetcorn	granturco	*grahntoorko*
sweet dreams	sogni d'oro	*sonyee doro!*
sweeteners	la saccarina	*lah sahkkahreenah*
swim (verb)	nuotare/fare il bagno	*nwotahray/fahray eel bahneeo*
swimming pool	piscina	*peesheenah*
swimming trunks	lo slip/il costume da bagno	*lo sleep/eel kostoomay dah bahneeo*
swindle	truffa	*trooffah*
switch	interruttore (m)	*eentayrroottoray*
synagogue	sinagoga	*seenahgogah*

T

table	tavolino	*tahvoleeno*
table tennis	ping-pong	*peeng-pong*
tablet	compressa	*komprayssah*
take (verb)	prendere	*prayndayray*
take (time) (verb)	durare	*doorahray*
talcum powder	talco	*tahlko*
talk (verb)	parlare	*pahrlahray*
tall	alto	*ahlto*
tampons	i tamponi	*ee tahmpony*
tanned	abbronzato	*ahbbronzahto*
tap	rubinetto	*roobeenaytto*
tap water	acqua del rubinetto	*ahkwah dayl roobeenaytto*
taste (verb)	assaggiare	*ahssahdjeeahray*
tax free shop	negozio duty-free	*naygotzeeo dootee-free*
taxi	il taxi	*eel tahxee*
taxi stand	posteggio dei taxi	*postedjeeo day tahxee*
tea	il tè	*eel tay*
teapot	teiera	*tayeeayrah*
teaspoon	cucchiaino	*kookkeeaheeno*
teat	tettarella	*tayttahrayllah*
telegram	il telegramma	*eel taylaygrahmmah*
telephoto lens	teleobiettivo	*taylayobeeaytteevo*
television set	il televisore	*eel taylayveezoray*
telex	il telex	*eel taylayx*
temperature	temperatura	*taympayrahtoorah*
temporary filling	otturazione provvisoria	*ottoorahtzeeonay provveezoreeah*
tender	tenero	*taynayro*
tennis (to play)	giocare a tennis	*jokahray ah taynnees*
tennis ball	palla da tennis	*pahllah dah taynnees*
tennis court	campo da tennis	*kahmpo dah taynnees*
tennis racket	racchetta da tennis	*rahkkayttah dah taynnees*
tenpin bowling	bowling	*boleeng*

tent	tenda	*tayndah*
tent peg	picchetto	*peekkaytto*
terminal (bus/tram)	il capolinea	*eel kahpoleenayah*
thank (verb)	ringraziare	*reengrahtzeeahray*
thank you	grazie	*grahtzeeay*
thank you very much	mille grazie	*meellay grahtzeeay*
thaw (verb)	sgelare	*sjaylahray*
the day after tomorrow	dopodomani	*dopodomahny*
theatre	teatro	*tayahtro*
theft	furto	*foorto*
there	là	*lah*
thermal bath	le terme	*lay tayrmay*
thermometer	termometro	*tayrmomaytro*
thick	spesso	*spaysso*
thief	ladro	*lahdro*
thigh	coscia	*koshah*
thin	magro	*mahgro*
things	roba	*robah*
think (verb)	pensare	*paynsahray*
third	terzo	*tayrtzo*
thirsty, to be	avere sete	*ahvayray saytay*
this afternoon	questo pomeriggio	*kwaysto pomayreedjo*
this evening	stasera	*stahsayrah*
this morning	stamattina	*stahmahtteenah*
thread	filo	*feello*
throat	gola	*golah*
throat lozenges	le pasticche per la gola	*lay pahsteekkay payr lah golah*
throw up (verb)	vomitare	*vomeetahray*
thunderstorm	il temporale	*eel taymporahlay*
Thursday	il giovedì	*eel jovaydee*
ticket	biglietto	*beellyetto*
tidy (verb)	mettere in ordine	*mayttayray een ordeenay*
tie	cravatta	*krahvahttah*
tights	la calzamaglia/il collant	*lah kahltzahmahlleeah/ eel kollahnt*

time	tempo	*taympo*
times	volte	*voltay*
timetable	orario	*orahreeo*
tin	lattina	*lahtteenah*
tip	mancia	*mahnchah*
tissues	i fazzoletti di carta	*ee fahtzolayttee dee kahrtah*
toast	il brindisi	*eel breendeezee*
toast (bread)	il pane tostato	*eel pahnay tostahto*
tobacco	tabacco	*tahbahkko*
toboggan	il toboga	*eel tobogah*
today	oggi	*odjee*
toe	dito (del piede)	*deeto (dayl peeayday)*
together	insieme	*eenseeaymay*
toilet	bagno/ gabinetto	*bahneeo/ gahbeenaytto*
toilet paper	carta igienica	*kahrtah eejayneekah*
toilet seat	sedile del water	*saydeellay dayl vahtayr*
toiletries	gli articoli da toletta	*lly ahrteekoly dah tolayttah*
tomato	pomodoro	*pomodoro*
tomato ketchup	il ketchup	*eel kaytchoop*
tomato purée	salsina di pomodoro	*sahlseenah dee pomodoro*
tomato sauce	sugo di pomodoro	*soogo dee pomodoro*
tomorrow	domani	*domahnee*
tongue	lingua	*leengwah*
tonic water	acqua tonica	*ahkwah toneekah*
tonight	stanotte	*stahnottay*
too much	troppo	*troppo*
tools	gli arnesi	*lly ahrnaysee*
tooth	il dente	*eel dayntay*
toothache	il mal di denti	*eel mahl dee dayntee*
toothbrush	lo spazzolino da denti	*lo spahtzoleeno dah dayntee*
toothpaste	dentifricio	*daynteefreecheeo*
toothpick	lo stuzzicadenti	*lo stootzeekahdayntee*
top up (verb)	riempire	*reeaympeeray*
total	totale	*totahlay*
tough	duro	*dooro*
tour	giro della città	*jeero dayllah cheettah*

tour guide	accompagnatore (m) turistico	*ahkkompahneeahtoray tooreesteeko*
tourist class	la classe turistica	*lah klahssay tooreesteekah*
Tourist Information office	ufficio informazioni turistiche	*ooffeecho eenformahtzeeonee tooreesteekay*
tourist menu	il menù turistico	*eel maynoo tooreesteeko*
tow (verb)	trainare	*traheenahray*
tow cable	cavo di traino	*kahvo dee traheeno*
towel	asciugamano	*ahshoogahmahno*
tower	la torre	*lah torray*
town	città	*cheettah*
toys	i giocattoli	*ee jokahttolee*
traffic	traffico	*trahffeeko*
traffic light	semaforo	*saymahforo*
trailer tent	il carrello tenda	*eel kahrrayllo tayndah*
train	treno	*trayno*
train ticket	biglietto (del treno)	*beellyaytto (dayltrayno)*
train timetable	orario ferroviario	*orahreeo fayrroveeahreeo*
translate (verb)	tradurre	*trahdoorray*
travel (verb)	viaggiare	*veeahdjahray*
travel agent	agenzia viaggi	*ahjayntzeeah veeahdjee*
travel guide	guida turistica	*gweedah tooreesteekah*
traveller	il viaggiatore	*eel veeahdjahtoray*
traveller's cheque	assegno turistico	*ahssayneeo tooreesteeko*
treacle/syrup	melassa/lo sciroppo di melassa	*maylahssah/lo sheeroppo dee maylahssah*
treatment	trattamento	*trahttahmaynto*
triangle	triangolo	*treeahngolo*
trim (verb)	accorciare	*ahkkorchahray*
trip	gita/viaggio	*jeetah/veeahdjo*
trousers/shorts	i pantaloni (lunghi, corti)	*ee pahntahlony (loongee/kortee)*
trout	trota	*trotah*
trunk call	interurbana	*eentayroorbahnah*

trunk code	prefisso	*prayfeesso*
trustworthy	fidato	*feedahto*
try on (verb)	provare	*provahray*
tube	tubetto	*toobaytto*
Tuesday	il martedì	*eel mahrtaydee*
tumble drier	asciugatore	*ahshoogahtoray*
tuna	tonno	*tonno*
tunnel	galleria	*gahllayreeah*
turn	volta	*voltah*
TV	la TV	*lah TeeVoo*
tweezers	pinzetta	*peentzayttah*
tyre (bicycle)	il copertone	*eel kopayrtonay*
tyre pressure	la pressione delle gomme	*lah praysseeonay dayllay gommay*

U

ugly	brutto	*brootto*
umbrella	ombrello	*ombrayllo*
under	giù/sotto	*joo/sotto*
underground	il metrò	*eel maytro*
underground railway system	metropolitana	*maytropoleetahnah*
underground station	la stazione del metrò	*lah stahtzeeonay dayl maytro*
underpants	le mutande	*lay mootahnday*
understand (verb)	capire	*kahpeeray*
underwear	biancheria intima	*beeahnkayreeah eenteemah*
undress (verb)	spogliarsi	*spollyahrsi*
unemployed	disoccupato	*deesokkoopahto*
uneven	ineguale	*eenaygwahlay*
university	università	*ooneevayrseetah*
unleaded	senza piombo	*saynzah peeombo*
urgent	urgente	*oorjayntay*
urgently	d'urgenza	*doorjayntzah*
urine	orina	*oreenah*

| use (verb) | usare | *oozahray* |
| usually | il più delle volte | *eel peeoo dayllay voltay* |

V

vacate (verb)	lasciare libero/a	*lahshahray leebayro/ah*
vaccinate (verb)	vaccinare	*vahtcheenahray*
vagina	vagina	*vahjeenah*
vaginal infection	infezione vaginale (f)	*eenfetzeeoonay vahjeenahlay*
valid	valido	*vahleedo*
valley	la valle	*lah vahllay*
valuable	prezioso	*praytzeeozo*
van	il furgone	*eel foorgonay*
vanilla	vaniglia	*vahneellyah*
vase	vaso	*vahzo*
vaseline	vaselina	*vahzayleenah*
veal	vitello	*veetayllo*
vegetable soup	il minestrone	*eel meenaystronay*
vegetables	verdura	*vayrdoorah*
vegetarian	vegetariano	*vayjaytahreeahno*
vein	vena	*vaynah*
vending machine	il distributore automatico	*eel deestreebootoray ahootomahteeko*
venereal disease	malattia venerea	*mahlahtteeah vaynayrayah*
via	per	*payr*
video recorder	il videoregistratore	*eel veedayorayjeestrahtoray*
video tape	videocassetta	*veedaeeokahssayttah*
view	il panorama	*eel pahnorahmah*
village	il paese	*eel pahaysay*
visa	visto	*veesto*
visit (verb)	visitare	*veezeetahray*
visit	visita	*veezeetah*
vitamins, vitamin tablets	le vitamine	*lay veetahmeenay*
volcano	vulcano	*voolkahno*
volleyball	pallavolo	*pahllahvolo*
vomit (verb)	vomitare	*vomeetahray*

W

wait (verb)	aspettare	*ahspayttahray*
waiter	il cameriere	*eel kahmayreeayray*
waiting room	sala d'attesa	*sahlah dahttayzah*
waitress	cameriera	*kahmayreeayrah*
wake up (verb)	svegliare	*svayllyahray*
Wales	Galles	*Gahllays*
walk	passeggiata/ giro a piedi	*pahssaydjeeahtah/ jeero ah peeaydee*
walk (verb)	fare due passi	*fahray dooay pahssee*
wallet	il portafoglio	*eel portahfollyo*
wardrobe	guardaroba	*gwahrdahrobah*
warn (verb)	avvisare/chiamare	*ahvveezahray/keeahmahray*
warning	avviso	*ahvveezo*
wash	lavare	*lahvahray*
washing-powder	detersivo	*daytayrseevo*
washing	bucato	*bookahto*
washing line	corda da bucato	*kordah dah bookahto*
washing machine	la lavatrice	*lah lahvahtreechay*
wasp	vespa	*vayspah*
water	acqua	*ahkwah*
water ski (verb)	fare lo sci nautico	*fahray lo shee nahooteeko*
waterfall	cascata	*kahskahtah*
waterproof	impermeabile (m)	*eempayrmayahbeellay*
wave-pool	piscina con movimento a onda marina	*peesheenah kon moveemaynto ah ondah mahreenah*
way	modo	*modo*
way (on the)	per strada	*payr strahdah*
way	la direzione	*lah deeraytzeeonay*
we	noi	*noee*
weak	debole	*daybolay*
weather	tempo	*taympo*
weather forecast	bollettino meteorologico	*bollaytteeno maytayorolodjeeko*

wedding	le nozze	*lay notzay*
Wednesday	il mercoledì	*eel mayrkolaydee*
week	settimana	*saytteemahnah*
weekend	il fine-settimana	*eel feenaysaytteemahnah*
weekend duty	servizio di fine-settimana	*sayrveetzeeo dee feenay-saytteemahnah*
welcome	benvenuto	*baynvaynooto*
well	bene	*baynay*
west	ovest (m)	*ovayst*
wet/damp	umido	*oomeedo*
wetsuit	muta	*mootah*
what/how?	come?	*komay?*
what?	che (cosa)?	*kay (kosah)?*
wheel	ruota	*rwotah*
wheelchair	sedia a rotelle	*saydeeah ah rotayllay*
when?	quando?	*kwahndo?*
where?	dove?	*dovay?*
which?	quale?	*kwahlay?*
whipped cream	panna montata	*pahnnah montahtah*
white	bianco	*beeahnko*
who?	chi?	*kee?*
wholemeal	integrale	*eentaygrahlay*
wholemeal bread	il pane integrale	*eel pahnay eentaygrahlay*
why?	perchè?	*payrkay?*
wide-angle lens	il grandangolare	*eel grahndahngolahray*
widow	vedova	*vaydovah*
widower	vedovo	*vaydovo*
wife	la moglie	*lah mollyay*
wind	vento	*vaynto*
windbreak	paravento	*pahrahveento*
window (car)	portiera	*porteeayrah*
window	finestrino/finestra	*feenaystreeno/feenaystrah*
window pane	vetro	*vaytro*
windscreen wiper	tergicristallo	*tayrjeekreestahllo*
wine	vino	*veeno*
wine list	lista dei vini	*leestah dayee veeny*
winter	inverno	*eenvayrno*

witness	il/la testimone	*eel/lah taysteemonay*
woman	donna	*donnah*
wood	legno	*layneeo*
wool	lana	*lahnah*
word	parola	*pahrolah*
work	lavoro	*lahvoro*
working day	giorno feriale	*jorno fayreeahlay*
worn	logoro	*logoro*
worried	preoccupato	*prayokkoopahto*
wound	ferita	*fayreetah*
wrap (verb)	incartare	*eenkahrtahray*
wrist	polso	*polso*
write (verb)	scrivere	*skreevayray*
write down (verb)	scrivere	*skreevayray*
writing pad	blocco	*blokko (ah*
(squared/lined)	(a quadretti/a righe)	*kwahdrayttee/ah reegay)*
writing paper	carta da lettere	*kahrtah dah layttayray*
written	per iscritto	*payr eeskreetto*
wrong	sbagliato	*sbahllyahto*

Y

yacht	lo yacht	*lo eeot*
year	anno	*ahnno*
yellow	giallo	*jahllo*
yes	sì	*see*
yes, please	volentieri	*volaynteeayree*
yesterday	ieri	*eeayree*
yoghurt	lo iogurt	*lo eeogoort*
you	Lei/tu	*layee/too*
you too	altrettanto	*ahltrayttahnto*
youth hostel	ostello della gioventù	*ostayllo dayllah jovayntoo*

Z

| zip | la chiusura lampo | *lah keeoozoorah lahmpo* |
| zoo | lo zoo | *lo dzo* |

There are two genders in Italian, masculine (m) and feminine (f). This applies to nouns, articles (the/a) and adjectives.

1 Definite article

The form of the definite article (English '**the**') depends on the sound at the beginning of the word following it:

	Singular	Plural
m	**il** bambino	**I** bambini (before a consonant)
m	**lo** zio/**lo** studente	**gli** zii/**gli** studenti (before z or s+consonant)
m	**l'**animale	**gli** animali (before a vowel)
f	**la** casa	**le** case (before a consonant)
f	**l'**amica	**le** amiche (before a vowel)

2 Indefinite article

Depending on the sound of the following word, the indefinite article (English '**a**' or '**an**',) is:

m	**un** bambino/ **un** animale	(before a consonant or a vowel)
m	**uno** zio/**uno** studente	(before z or s+consonant)
f	**una** casa	(before a consonant)
f	**un'**amica	(before a vowel)

The plural of the in definite article (English '**some**') are:

m	**dei** bambini	(before consonant)
m	**degli** zii/**degli** studenti	(before z or s+consonant)
f	**delle** bambine/ **delle** amiche	(before a consonant or a vowel)

3 Nouns

In general:

Nouns ending in **-o** are masculine. To form the plural change **-o** to **-i**: (vin**o**-vin**i**)

Nouns ending in **-a** are feminine. To form the plural change **-a** to **-e**: (birr**a**- birr**e**)

Nouns ending in **-e** are either masculine or feminine. Learn each individually. To form the plural change **-e** to **-i**: il pied**e** (**m**) **-i** pied**i**; la nott**e** (**f**) – le nott**i**

Some nouns are irregular:
la mano (hand) is feminine
il problema (problem) is masculine

Nouns ending in **-ista** can be either masculine or feminine:
il/la dentista; **il/la** pianista

4 Adjectives

Adjectives tend to go after the noun they refer to. They must agree with the noun they accompany, both in gender (masculine/feminine) and in number (singular/plural).

	Singular	Plural
m	**un ragazzo italiano**	**dei ragazzi italiani**
m	**uno studente italiano**	**degli studenti italiani**
(m	**un tavolo grande**	**dei tavoli grandi)**
f	**una ragazza italiana**	**delle ragazze italiane**
f	**una stanza grande**	**delle stanze grandi**
(f	**una stazione vicina**	**delle stazioni vicine)**

5 Possessive adjectives

A possessive adjective agrees in gender and in number with the noun whch follows it, and not with the 'owner' as in English. It is usually preceded by the definite article:

	masculine		feminine	
	singular	plural	singular	plural
my, mine	**il mio**	**i miei**	**la mia**	**le mie**
your, yours	**il tuo**	**i tuoi**	**la tua**	**le tue**
his, her, hers, its	**il suo**	**i suoi**	**la sua**	**le sue**
our, ours	**il nostro**	**i nostri**	**la nostra**	**le nostre**
your, yours	**il vostro**	**i vostri**	**la vostra**	**le vostre**
their, theirs	**il loro**	**i loro**	**la loro**	**le loro**

6 Personal pronouns

Since verb endings are normally sufficient to indicate who is doing the action, io, tu, lei, lui, etc. are only used for emphasis or to avoid confusion.

I	**io**
you (singular and familiar)	**tu**
he	**lui**
she,you (formal)	**lei**
we	**noi**
voi (you, plural)	**voi**
they	**loro**

7 Verbs

Regular verbs follow one of three patterns, depending on their endings in the infinitive.

	-are	-ere	-ire
infinitive	comprare	prendere	dormire
	(to buy)	(to take)	(to sleep)
(io)	compro	prendo	dormo
(tu)	compri	prendi	dormi
(lui/lei)	compra	prende	dorme
(noi)	compriamo	prendiamo	dormiamo
(voi)	comprate	prendete	dormite
(loro)	comprano	prendono	dormono